"The world has become overwhelmingly complex, and new models of leadership are required. In *Leadership on a Blockchain*, Dr. Corbett expertly, succinctly, and with deep insight details the future of leadership: distributed, connected, and networked."

Professor George Siemens, *Centre for Change and Complexity in Learning, University of South Australia, Australia*

"Dr. Corbett's idea of *Leadership on a Blockchain* is a winning model for new-age leaders. It promotes the idea of distributed leadership, which is key to building the right culture in the digital age. The book is deeply strategic and highly actionable."

Dheeraj Sinha, *CEO, Leo Burnett South Asia; Chairman, BBH, India*

"*Leadership on a Blockchain* is a rallying cry to redefine leadership: no longer personified in a singular senior individual; it is instead an organization-wide system of distributed decision-making, expertise, and empowerment. With the accelerated economic, technological, and social change, never has this new idea of leadership been more critical to success."

Justin Halim, *Expert Partner, Bain & Company Southeast Asia, Singapore*

Leadership on a Blockchain

Leadership on a Blockchain: What Asia Can Teach Us About Networked Leadership is an authoritative text that goes to the foremost digitally connected markets of the world in Asia, and accounts for how leaders and teams are exercising leadership Darwinism to adapt for agility and connectivity.

The book begins by offering a contextual grounding for new leadership ideas to emerge. It contends that a "new geography of leadership" is unfolding as the world shifts away from unified globalist ideology and a dominant Western view of leadership. It moves on to describe how Asia is uniquely placed to become the leadership sandbox for the future. It accounts for how leaders and teams are exercising leadership Darwinism to adapt for agility and connectivity. To facilitate learning for the readers, this book includes creative features such as the following:

- An abbreviated history of significant leadership milestones in the last century
- A leadership manifesto for the digital age
- A practitioners' starter kit to reimagining leadership in their organizations.

Leaving behind the typical discourse of leadership anchored in power, control, and hierarchy, it offers a provocative call to all businesspeople to apply the principles of one of the most innovative technologies – blockchain – to reimagine leadership for transparency, trust, and distributed decision-making. The book concludes by distilling critical lessons for global leaders to take forward and lead a revolution in their own organizations.

Sharing first-person accounts from leaders and their teams in China, Singapore, India, and Indonesia, and combining this with insights from the author's own research, *Leadership on a Blockchain* will be of use to leaders around the world looking to transform their own leadership. It will also be of interest to academics and students of leadership, change management, organizational behavior, and cultural studies.

Dr. Frederique Covington Corbett is a lecturer at Pepperdine and Berkeley University who also sits on the Board of Directors of EFFIE Worldwide, which champions the practice of marketing effectiveness globally. She holds a PhD in Global Leadership and Change.

She is a senior executive who has held many top-level leadership positions and has been recognized as an innovative thinker, trailblazer, and thought leader at the intersection of leadership, technology, and culture. Most recently, she was the SVP, Chief Global Brand and Integrated Marketing Officer at Visa. Previously, she has held senior marketing positions at Microsoft and Twitter and has also been the Managing Partner of the Ogilvy Bates WPP advertising group.

Leadership: Research and Practice

Handbook of International and Cross-Cultural Leadership Research Processes
Perspectives, Practice, Instruction
Yulia Tolstikov-Mast, Franziska Bieri, and Jennie L. Walker

Deepening the Leadership Journey
Nine Elements of Leadership Mastery
Al Bolea and Leanne Atwater

Donald Trump in Historical Perspective
Dead Precedents
Edited by Michael Harvey

Intentional Leadership
Becoming a Trustworthy Leader
Karen E. Mishra and Aneil K. Mishra

Leadership and Virtues
Understanding and Practicing Good Leadership
Edited by Toby P. Newstead and Ronald E. Riggio

Leadership Mindsets for Adaptive Change
The Flux 5
Sharon Ravitch and Liza Herzog

Leadership on a Blockchain
What Asia Can Teach Us About Networked Leadership
Frederique Covington Corbett

For more information about this series, please visit: www.routledge.com/Leadership-Research-and-Practice/book-series/leadership

Leadership on a Blockchain

What Asia Can Teach Us About Networked Leadership

Frederique Covington Corbett

Routledge
Taylor & Francis Group
NEW YORK AND LONDON

Designed cover image: © Getty

First published 2024
by Routledge
605 Third Avenue, New York, NY 10158

and by Routledge
4 Park Square, Milton Park, Abingdon, Oxon, OX14 4RN

Routledge is an imprint of the Taylor & Francis Group, an informa business

Library of Congress Cataloging-in-Publication Data
Names: Corbett, Frederique Covington, author.
Title: Leadership on a blockchain: what Asia can teach us about networked leadership / Frederique Covington Corbett.
Description: New York, NY: Routledge, 2023. |
Series: Leadership: research and practice |
Includes bibliographical references and index.
Identifiers: LCCN 2023010804 (print) | LCCN 2023010805 (ebook) |
ISBN 9781032506326 (hardback) | ISBN 9781032506319 (paperback) |
ISBN 9781003399377 (ebook)
Subjects: LCSH: Leadership—Asia. | Business networks—Asia. |
Strategic alliances (Business)—Asia.
Classification: LCC HD57.7 .C66897 2023 (print) | LCC HD57.7 (ebook) |
DDC 658.4/092095—dc23/eng/20230322
LC record available at https://lccn.loc.gov/2023010804
LC ebook record available at https://lccn.loc.gov/2023010805

ISBN: 978-1-032-50632-6 (hbk)
ISBN: 978-1-032-50631-9 (pbk)
ISBN: 978-1-003-39937-7 (ebk)

DOI: 10.4324/9781003399377

Typeset in Sabon
by codeMantra

Contents

About the Author

Dr. Frederique Covington Corbett is a senior executive passionate about teamwork and the pursuit of transformative ideas. She has held many top-level leadership positions and has been recognized as an innovative thinker, trailblazer, and thought leader at the intersection of leadership, technology, and culture.

Most recently, Frederique was the Senior Vice President, Chief Global Brand and Integrated Marketing Officer at Visa. Beforehand, she held senior marketing positions at Microsoft and Twitter. Earlier in her career, Frederique rose through the ranks of the agency world as the Managing Partner of the Ogilvy Bates WPP advertising group.

Frederique has a multicultural background as a European, with extensive working experience in Asia and North America. She has been recognized as a leading voice in marketing as an influential and purposeful marketer. Furthermore, her scholarly work has provided a unique academic lens to her practitioner's background. In 2009, she was awarded the Grand Prix Atticus Award for best original thinking amongst WPP firms globally for "The Dictionary of Change." Most recently, she completed a Doctor of Philosophy in Global Leadership and Change, studying the impact of culture and technology on leadership.

Frederique lectures at Pepperdine University and the University of California, Berkeley and currently sits on the Board of Directors of EFFIE Worldwide, which champions the practice of marketing effectiveness globally.

Foreword

Don Tapscott

In 2016, Alex Tapscott and I wrote *Blockchain Revolution and the Timing Was Right.* It seems the world was looking for a well-researched and readable explanation of how blockchain technology would change business, money, and society. The book did become an instant bestseller, and even touted as the iconic piece "to survive and thrive in the next wave of technology-driven disruption."[1] To this day, it is the best-selling book on the topic, and it led to other impactful initiatives such as our widely watched TED Talks, INSEAD educational programs on Coursera, and the launch of the Blockchain Research Institute.

In Chapter 11, entitled "Leadership for the Next Era," we started to think about the implications of blockchain, and radical openness, distributed power, and participation would foster innovative governance models and a new philosophy for leadership. The deep structures and architecture of the firm would change, we argued, and new decentralized models would emerge. We argued that those who would lead the transformation would stray far from the traditional norms of leadership based on hierarchy and power and the dominant paradigm of the industrial age. We also discussed how entrenched beneficiaries of the old order would be hard to displace. To govern, lead, and manage these new models, we would need to reinvent management science and turn the old concept of the industrial age leader on its head. The most effective leaders would not be the so-called "visionaries" who sell their strategy down and motivate their people to follow them. Rather, a new kind of collaborative leader would emerge, one that might be based on the core principles of blockchain itself, outlined in the book.

I'm delighted to report that this topic has been taken to the next level. *Leadership on a Blockchain* provides evidence that this profound leadership transformation is underway, enabling important new opportunities for value creation and entrepreneurship. The book documents a significant departure from the heroic underlying concept of leadership and the conventional culture of governance. Central to these new approaches is the belief that leading is the responsibility of everyone, not just a designated leader, and that there are no more so-called "followers." The design principles of the Blockchain Revolution are put to the test with progressive leaders and teams demonstrating distributed power, inclusion, shared ownership, integrity, and trust. Based on a substantial research project and data set, Dr. Corbett presents new leadership and governance approaches that embody the philosophical ethos of blockchain, its decentralized decision-making model, instant communications, peer-to-peer collaborative work groups, and open business architecture. Against this backdrop, workers are demanding greater equality in the leadership dynamic and calling for the end of a command-and-control approach to increase their rights and agency. This is especially true among the younger generation, who have radically different expectations of leaders and are exercising workforce activism for greater transparency, honesty, humanity, and purpose in organizations.

In our digital age, *Leadership on a Blockchain* is a must-read for anyone who wants to understand how blockchain technology, its spirit, implicit ideology, and philosophical tenets can affect leadership and, in turn, how a new leadership approach is required for new decentralized business models. While the technology is facing massive headwinds and serious challenges, this assessment of how it affects leadership can help us reimagine the architecture of the firm and those driving value in it. Victor Hugo said there is nothing so powerful as an idea whose time has come. In the case of leadership, the pull for a networked understanding of our institutions and human behaviors is irresistible.

Read on, learn, enjoy, and prosper.
Don Tapscott C.M.
CEO, The Tapscott Group Inc.
Adjunct Professor, INSEAD
Co-founder of The Blockchain Research Institute
Chancellor Emeritus, Trent University

Don Tapscott is CEO of the Tapscott Group, executive chairman of the Blockchain Research Institute, and one of the world's leading authorities on the impact of technology on business and society. He has authored more than 16 books, including *Wikinomics: How Mass Collaboration Changes Everything* (with Anthony Williams), which has been translated into more than 25 languages. He coined the term, "The Digital Economy," in his 1994 book of that title, and many of his big ideas are part of the business vernacular today. In 2016, with his son Alex, he co-authored *Blockchain*

Revolution: How the Technology Behind Bitcoin and Other Cryptocurrencies Is Changing the World, now translated in over 20 languages. His TED talk on the topic has received over 7 million views in English alone. In 2019, when ranked the #2 living business thinker, Don was inducted into the Thinkers50 Hall of Fame. He is an adjunct professor at INSEAD and former two-term chancellor of Trent University in Canada.

Note

1 Clay Christensen, the late Harvard Business School Professor and best-selling author.

Series Editor Foreword

For those of us who teach leadership to Gen Z students, or for parents of these young adults, we know that they think differently about the world and about leadership. Past generations viewed leadership in heroic terms (the Silent Generation, Baby Boomers) and looked to top-level leaders to get things done. Gen X and Millennials saw leadership in visionary entrepreneurs and noted NGO leaders who promoted social change on a grand scale. The generation now entering the workforce sees that leadership is in all of us, working collectively. Fortunately, recent leadership scholarship is catching up, with greater attention paid to distributed, shared, and networked leadership. There is also growing recognition of leadership's complexity. Read on, in this excellent addition to our book series, and all of this will become much clearer. With the publication of this book, *Leadership on a Blockchain*, Dr. Frederique Covington Corbett helps us look directly at the future of the study and practice of leadership. Solidly grounded in the author's research, and her career experience and global perspective, we get a glimpse into the future of leadership in organizations and societies. The implications for leadership research and practice are enormous.

Ronald E. Riggio, PhD
Henry R. Kravis Professor of Leadership and Organizational Psychology
Kravis Leadership Institute
Claremont McKenna College

Acknowledgments

Frederique Covington Corbett

This book would not exist without the infinite wisdom of my study participants who took part in my original PhD research study in 2020. All the ideas presented here are theirs, as well as the new language they proposed to describe the leadership dynamics they are witnessing and experiencing firsthand. For reasons of confidentiality, my study participants shall remain anonymous, but I wish to express my deep gratitude to the 42 individuals I had the chance to interview and who granted me their time and insights. I would also like to commend them for having the courage to go against the status quo, defying organizational, societal, and cultural norms that have confined leadership to a formulaic and often archaic genre. If leadership has a chance to look, sound, and feel different, it is because they are rewriting the rules and applying an entrepreneurial and network metaphor to set it free.

I am indebted to all the people with whom I have had the chance to practice leadership during my career and who helped me realize that no one is a follower but rather a co-founder, partner, supporter, cheerleader, counselor, coach, and reverse mentor. Together, we have experimented with and tried many of the dynamics described in this book. Thanks to my professional *in situ* practice, my beliefs grew stronger, my willingness to fail and try again turned into resilience, and my outlook became laser-focused on team dynamics to reinvent a more generous and fulfilling approach to leadership that recognizes the critical role of every single person.

It was a heavy load to lift the references and ideas of this book into a concise narrative that can engage all readers. My heartfelt appreciation is extended to Dr. Roda and Dr. Nielsen for their writing support and editing guidance on this book.

I am infinitely grateful to my children, Naia and Max, who inspire my lifelong desire to become a better leader and leave a legacy of new ideas to pass on to the next generation of leaders. Finally, my deepest love and gratitude go to my husband, Julian, for his willingness to let me disappear in my papers and for his ruthless critique and editing of my manuscript.

Preface

Frederique Covington Corbett

Leadership is a concept as old as humanity itself, with early mentions of the English word "leader" dating back to the year 1300 (Bass, 1981). Much has been written on leadership theories, the enactment of leadership practices, the profiles of iconic leaders, and their different leadership styles. Leadership is a perennial subject of study, which has resulted in hundreds of definitions and extensive literature from scholars and practitioners. Counting all formats, Amazon currently offers 60,000 books with the word "leadership" in their titles, and it is estimated that four new books come out every day on the topic (Gopalakrishnan, 2022). Leadership fascinates – it generates a plethora of opinions, self-appointed experts, definitions, theories, and frameworks. Stogdill (1974) remarked that the definitions of leadership were as numerous as those who had attempted to articulate them. For his part, Burns (1978, p. 2) concluded that leadership was "one of the most observed and least understood phenomena on earth."

So why another book on leadership? Despite the vast amount of literature on the topic, many of the ideas presented are variants of a similar discourse that reinforces heroic leadership (Bradford & Cohen, 1998), celebrating a solo leader with the ability to influence others through extraordinary abilities rather than through a leadership system. In addition to this highly individualistic representation, leadership also lacks diversity. The *Harvard Business Review* list of "11 Books Every Young Leader Should Read" (Coleman, 2012) only includes titles written by men. This canon of leadership greatness omits women's voices and perspectives from other major regions of the world, such as Asia. Finally, leadership is changing rapidly. For the last decade, leadership has undergone a metamorphosis, and since the global pandemic, further transformed. What is available on the topic has not kept pace with the realities of how teams are now self-organizing to deal with uncertainty and change, and little is documented on the technology and network imperative that modern leadership requires. This book aims to break with many of the prevalent myths of leadership and usher in a more progressive version of what leadership looks like, reflective of trends emerging in Asia.

As a senior executive who worked in Asia for 15 years, I had a front-row seat to how leadership was in a tug of war between traditional modalities of practice (disempowering, hierarchical, and Western dominant) and newer models enacted by the younger generations (networked, decentralized, and culturally relevant). I decided to take matters into my own hands and search for new leadership knowledge, perspectives, and inspiration. In my mid-40s, I returned to school to complete a doctoral program in Global Leadership and Change. After several years of research and completing my PhD, colleagues, teammates, leadership coaches, and trainers often called on me to share what I had learned. I decided to translate my dissertation (Corbett, 2021) into this book, compelled by challenges that remained unheard and unaddressed:

- **Most of the leadership literature is similar and reinforces biases.**

Books on leadership primarily consist of leader autobiographies promoting age-old and disproven leadership theories based on personality, traits, and style. These approaches reinforce a view of leadership founded on power, warfare metaphors, and power imbalance between those who lead and those who follow. The language of leadership in the literature has not evolved for centuries; it still talks of "leaders" and "followers" and presents a two-class system where inequality is not only assumed but encouraged. This book anchors its approach in defining leadership as a relationship of mutual importance and purpose. It also offers a new language, based on verbatim accounts collected from real leaders and teams in the field, to recast the leadership dynamic.

- **New leadership understanding requires both theory and practice.**

Most books on leadership are either too academic, with theories that are hard to understand and often unusable, or filled with practical advice with no research backing. This book has a concern for both theory and practice, aiming to bring together two worlds that typically do not intersect. Practitioners can learn from the serious academic research presented in this book, while academics can learn from the experience of the practitioners who shared their insights in this qualitative exploration. In truth, one must walk the talk to be a credible contributor to leadership. Leadership does not work based on frameworks and models alone, nor can it be practiced without conceptual understanding. This book aims to bridge the divide between research and practice by imparting new knowledge on leadership from theoretical research and applied skill sets that demonstrate new human and social behavioral patterns. With this synergistic relationship, one field can inform the other, and academics and practitioners will be able to enhance and guide their practices based on newly established learnings. Hopefully, the material in this book will be of interest to scholars and business leaders alike.

- **Leadership training is a far cry from leadership practice.**

Leadership development is mainly focused on influence, power, persuasion, decision-making, and conflict management. What about relationship building, connection, teams, distributed influence, crowdsourcing of ideas, and shared vision? When leadership is done right, it feels right, and it is rarely about coming out on top but creating and winning *with* others. The current approach to leadership capacity building is highly inadequate and focused on individual competencies rather than the process of team building and managing a successful network effect with others. Thus, gaining more insights into the success of this collective enterprise is the most critical and under-researched aspect of leadership. This book aims to elucidate a greater understanding of the leadership dynamics of all those involved, the social interactions produced, and the possible emergence that occurs as a result.

- **Some leadership voices are never heard.**

The field of global leadership development has burgeoned with scholars responding to the need for frameworks and approaches guiding global talent management and addressing practitioners' growing interest in leadership programs across cultures; however, to date, the discussion has focused on a one-size-fits-all model for global leadership, anchored heavily in Western preconceptions. Despite the rise in the amount of scholarship on leadership, practitioners have been left with a one-sided view of what it means to lead. The dominant theories of leadership have been developed by Western thinkers, primarily from North America, introducing underlying cultural biases and assumptions (House & Javidan, 2004; Wilson, 2016). This book aims to present findings from the voices of leaders and their teams in Asia that break out of the dominant Western leadership paradigm and respond to evolving corporate organizational models and the needs of increasingly networked workers.

References

Bass, B. M. (1981). *Bass & Stogdill's handbook of leadership: Theory, research and managerial applications.* Collier Macmillan Publishers.

Bradford, D. L., & Cohen, A. R. (1998). *Power up: Transforming organizations through shared leadership* (1st ed.). John Wiley & Sons, Inc.

Burns, J. M. (1978). *Leadership*. Harper & Row.Coleman, J. (2012, October 11). 11 Books every young leader must read. *Harvard Business Review*. https://hbr.org/2012/10/11-books-every-young-leader-mu

Corbett, F. (2021). *Emergence of the connectivist leadership paradigm: A grounded theory study in the Asia region*. [Doctoral dissertation, Pepperdine]. Theses and Dissertations. 1194. https://digitalcommons.pepperdine.edu/etd/1194

Gopalakrishnan, R. (2022, March 15). Dimensions of leadership. *Business Standard*. https://www.business-standard.com/article/beyond-business/dimensions-of-leadership-122031500001_1.html

House, R. J., & Javidan, M. (2004). Overview of GLOBE. In R. J. House, P. J. Hanges, M. Javidan, P. W. Dorfman & V. Gupta (Eds.), *Culture, leadership, and organizations: The GLOBE study of 62 societies* (pp. 9–48). Sage Publications.

Stogdill, R. M. (1974). *Handbook of leadership: A survey of theory and research*. Free Press.

Wilson, S. (2016). *Thinking differently about leadership: A critical history of leadership studies*. Edward Elgar.

Introduction

Path to This Book

The source material for this book is a PhD dissertation I wrote while completing my Doctor of Philosophy on Global Leadership and Change at Pepperdine University in California. The original manuscript was published in 2021 and entitled "Emergence of the Connectivist Leadership paradigm: A grounded theory study in the Asia region" (Corbett, 2021). The study aimed to create and present a new leadership theory called "Connectivist Leadership" to advance the understanding of leadership based on leadership practices researched and documented in Asia. As previously noted, most of the leadership literature to date has come from Western thinkers who have standardized ideals about leadership based on certain cultural assumptions and implicit biases. Understanding emerging leadership dynamics from an Eastern perspective presented a real opportunity to contribute new knowledge and open fresh conversations.

While dissertations are highly specialized and contain frameworks and theories, a book is a different endeavor and has more of a storytelling approach. Books are geared toward general readers and need to make content easier to absorb and apply. My goal in writing this book, using my dissertation as source material, was to extract the most significant aspects of my findings and relay the voices of my research participants compellingly and truthfully. I also wanted to avoid overwhelming the reader with unnecessary details; therefore, this book is rich in verbatim accounts extracted as recorded in the original research. It focuses primarily on the findings of the qualitative research study I conducted with 42 people, using in-depth interviews split between 29 participants (leaders and teams in Asia) and 13 global leadership experts. My qualitative study aimed to explore a new form of leadership emerging in Asia by examining the lived experiences of individuals and groups who lead and are led in this region. In the book, I share with the reader the results of my analysis and how the findings can help reinvent our views and practices of leadership.

DOI: 10.4324/9781003399377-1

My original dissertation used the study findings to propose a new leadership theory called "Connectivist Leadership." Connectivism (Siemens, 2005a) is a learning theory that emphasizes the importance of networks and connectivity in acquiring and disseminating knowledge. This perspective can be applied to leadership by recognizing the role that networks play in developing and implementing leadership strategies. In the Connectivist approach to leadership, leaders can be viewed as nodes in a network. Their effectiveness is determined by their ability to connect with and leverage the network's resources (both human and digital). This perspective can help leaders understand the importance of building and maintaining strong relationships with their colleagues, employees, and other stakeholders. It can also provide insight into navigating complex and dynamic organizational environments. In this book, I have removed the more theoretical aspects of learning theories to focus on describing how the phenomenon I discovered affects the behaviors, feelings, and leadership practices of leaders and their teams.

My dissertation also included over 100 pages dedicated to an extensive literature review on global leadership in Chapter 2. I have summarized in a very light manner the findings from this secondary research to give the reader some background on the historical context surrounding leadership and evaluate how my work contributes to a new perspective. Most of the book's content is focused on presenting findings covered in my original Chapter 4 with the meta themes that emanated from participants' views and leadership experts.

I hope this book manages to translate my research in a thorough and entertaining way to strike a balance between the serious academic effort it represented and the genuinely new perspectives it uncovered. For those interested in reading my whole dissertation, you can find it at https://digitalcommons.pepperdine.edu/etd/1194/.

Research Overview

Though technical, it is essential to give at least a summary explanation of the research methodology behind this book. This information will make the results more meaningful and provide the necessary context for how the analysis was derived. The material presented in this book is sourced from a PhD dissertation completed in 2021. If, at times, the information presented feels a bit heavy, technical, or academic, it is because I have tried to stay as close as possible to my original work and extract the findings in a way that preserves the integrity of what I discovered and the voices of my participants. I based my conclusions on an extensive literature review, a quantitative research survey, and a qualitative research study. The qualitative research, which is the main foundation for this book, aimed to explore the integral social relationships and group behaviors of leaders and followers in Asia, where little exploration of leadership has been documented. Though this section might appeal more to those with a more academic interest, it will provide the needed background for any reader seeking to benefit from the practical results discussed in the subsequent sections.

The central research question for the original research inquiry was: "If, and to what extent, are leaders and teams shifting their understanding and practices of leadership, from a process led primarily by an individual to a system of shared and digitally connected relationships?" Three secondary questions guided the study:

1 What challenges do leaders in the Asia region face when leading teams?
2 What leadership approaches and paradigms (contrasting leader-centric versus team-centric) do leaders and teams use?
3 How do culture and technology influence the distribution of leadership enacted in the Asian context?

The qualitative study was grounded in an extensive literature review structured around three main themes: (1) exploring leadership within new *learning and knowledge* paradigms, (2) understanding emerging post-heroic leadership within new *organizational* paradigms, and (3) analyzing leadership beyond Western-centric *cultural* paradigms. The literature review drew on published material that illuminated the current state of the leadership field in theory and practice and intended to provide a foundation for a new leadership theory based on data collection. The conceptual framework for the study brought together perspectives on the evolution of learning and knowledge, the advancement of leadership through changes in organizational design, and an investigation of how culture impacts leadership. This review revealed a consistent parallel development between the three areas of learning, organizational design, and culture to that of leadership.

The literature review began with an analysis of how knowledge and meaning are acquired through theories of learning, tracing their systematic development alongside the advancement of leadership theory. Situating the evolution of leadership within contemporary educational thought provides a vehicle for understanding how the dominant values of their time mutually influenced educational and leadership theories. The literature review evaluated the progress of prevailing learning theories from traditional learning theories (Mann, 1853; Swett, 1876) to behaviorism (Pavlov, 1927; Skinner, 1938; Thorndike, 1913; Tolman, 1932; Watson, 1930), cognitivism (Bruner, 1961; Köhler & Winter, 1925; Piaget, 1952), constructivism (Bruner, 1961; Dewey, 1922; Knowles et al., 2005a; Piaget, 1977; Vygotsky & Cole, 1978), humanism (Bandura, 1977; Barth, 1988;

Maslow, 1943), and connectivism (Downes, 2007, 2008; Siemens, 2005b, 2006).

Researching the evolution of educational theories of learning in correspondence with leadership theories presented a picture of how new ideas about learning influenced new ideas about leading. Shifting roles for learners and teachers open new avenues for conceptualizing evolved roles for leaders and followers in the future. This part of the review provided the background for the foundational premise of the research problem, which proposed to attach a modern learning theory – connectivism – to leadership and explore if, and to what extent, it can describe a new leadership phenomenon known as Connectivist Leadership (Corbett & Spinello, 2020).

The second portion of the literature review refined the research problem and study purpose by relating leadership advancement through examining changing organizational structures. Organizational models presented in the conceptual framework included mechanistic organizational systems and legacy leader-centric leadership with a review of centralized organizations (Smith, 2008), scientific organizations (Fayol, 1916; Taylor, 1911), and bureaucratic organizations (Drucker, 2006; Locke, 1968; Weber, 1979). Then, organic systems and emerging post-heroic leadership were detailed with a review of social organizations (Barnard, 1968; Davis & Lawrence, 1977; Galbraith, 2016; Trist, 1981) and agile organizations (De Smet et al., 2019; Hock, 2000; Kreitzer et al., 2015; Laloux, 2014; Mintzberg, 1979; Robertson, 2015; Snow, 2015; Ulieru et al., 2002). As with the study of learning models, leadership was seen to change alongside the evolution of organization design, leading to emerging post-heroic leadership approaches within new organizational paradigms.

The final portion of the review examined culture and leadership, drawing into focus the biases that have guided our understanding of leadership, given it has been based primarily on Western-centric cultural paradigms. It is clear that there is a close relationship between culture and leadership. Leadership models cannot be understood apart from the cultural environment in which they are employed (House & Javidan, 2004). Leadership significantly shapes the culture by directing people's decisions about how to solve problems, survive, and thrive. As such, "leadership is involved in the creation of the culture" (Schein, 2017, p. 15).

Cultural models presented in the conceptual framework included Western-centric leadership models and theories (Blunt & Jones, 1997; Brewster & Bournois, 1991; Hofstede, 1980; House & Javidan, 2004; Rost, 1991; Wilson, 2013). According to Foucault (1972, p. 191), "something like a world-view... a certain structure of thought" has prevailed at any given time in the study of leadership, shaping what has been considered acceptable, thinkable, relevant, and sayable about this topic. The Western leadership model holds many biases not shared by other cultures and is heavily dominated by two central issues: power and morality. It tends toward individualism rather than collective action and presents assumptions of rationality specific to the United States (House & Javidan, 2004). Since the turn of the nineteenth century, leadership studies have increased. Yet, the nature of the knowledge produced remains limited because it has been focused on a culturally conditioned set of ideas that favor the heroic leader-centric paradigm that depends upon a single, charismatic visionary. Western human resource management exerts a type of "cultural hegemony" (Brewster & Bournois, 1991). Similarly, the US management and leadership theory "has become a cultural and ideological imperative" (Blunt & Jones, 1997, p. 8).

Rost (1991, p. 7) explained that part of the appeal of leadership as a field of study is its "mythological significance" throughout history. He argued that leadership is a symbolic story in America meant to reconcile people with their harsh living conditions. At the start of the United States, leadership gave meaning to immigrants' search for survival through heroes they could look up to and leadership secrets they could learn. As America became economically challenged by other world economies in the 1980s, leadership turned to the search for excellence. The emphasis of leadership was placed on power and prestige as a vehicle to reestablish America's global dominance (Rost, 1991). Hofstede et al. (2010, p. 508) remarked that some "societies romanticize the construct of leadership as is in the case of the US where leaders are given exceptional privileges, accorded high status, and are held in great esteem." Understanding the underlying assumptions embedded in the current Western-centric leadership literature is essential. Leadership is more than an academic discipline; it contains the manifestation of culture.

Methodology

Any research study requires a plan of instrumentation to determine the data necessary to answer the research question and collect and analyze the data once gathered. Before my dissertation, I undertook a quantitative study, which was published under *The Rise of Connectivist Leadership* (Corbett et al., 2018). This research provided the foundational hypotheses for my PhD study. This earlier study isolated the criteria underpinning the Connectivist Leadership theory under current investigation in my dissertation. An initial research phase on Connectivist Leadership was conceived and developed in early 2018. This quantitative descriptive and correlational study, including a total sample of 317 individuals, was carried out in the United States and the Asia-Pacific region, in this case, India, Malaysia, Singapore, and Australia. The research was based on a 26-question survey comprised of demographic characteristics and an exploration of personal values, emotional intelligence, attitudes toward work, technology orientations, leadership orientations, leadership principles, and views on the future of leadership.

The study explored the extent to which leadership orientations were changing from the classically held assumptions of authority, power, control, and hierarchy toward more collective and connected approaches, thanks to, and with, technology and network connectivity. The study also explored differences in leadership and technology orientations between respondents residing in the United States and those in Asia. Initial results from the main study were presented at The Asian Conference on the Social Sciences (ACSS2020) in May 2020 (Corbett & Sweeney, 2020). The report analyzed just one independent variable (geographic location) and one dependent variable (leadership orientations) to isolate the areas of significance related to a new collective and connected leadership paradigm.

One of the significant hypotheses this earlier quantitative study validated was that leadership orientations were evolving from the traditional views of power, authority, control, and hierarchy to a system of shared relationships grounded in connecting people, the use of technology, and the shifting of information sources to create collective influence. This was true across the entire study sample. Furthermore, leadership orientations were also more pronounced in certain attributes depending on the geographic location. Respondents from the Asia region displayed statistically significant results compared to those in the United States, as having a much stronger orientation toward more connected and collective forms of leadership.

Based on the data set presented in the research (Corbett & Sweeney, 2020), it was possible to classify the leadership orientations expressed by respondents into three groups: (1) traditional, (2) status quo, and (3) emerging. Traditional leadership orientations were derived from respondents' agreement to leadership orientations anchored on power (leadership as defined through authority, power, control, and hierarchy), on traits (leadership as defined by personal traits), and on skills (leadership as defined by possessing the right skillset). Status quo leadership orientations were derived from respondents' agreement to leadership defined through common goals (leadership as the common purposes of leaders and followers) and the quality of the relationship between leaders and followers (leadership as the relationship between the leader and the follower; leadership as the quality of the networking relationship of all those involved). Emerging leadership orientations were derived from respondents' agreement to leadership defined through the distribution of influence (leaders and followers share the leadership process; followers can influence the leadership process as much as leaders), connectivity (leadership is a process of connecting people and information sources to create collective influence), and inclusivity (leaders need to empower multiple groups, not just individuals to allow for an inclusive diversity of voices).

This previous quantitative study established validity for the Connectivist Leadership phenomenon at multiple levels: content validity (measuring the critical aspects of Connectivist Leadership through leadership orientations as one dimension), concurrent validity (correlating the results of respondents in the United States versus those in Asia), and construct validity (establishing different views of leadership based on specific criteria). This instrument also presented strong reliability. Cronbach Alpha measured 0.761 with all ten leadership orientations grouped regardless of primary components. When the data were split between respondents in the United States and those in Asia, Cronbach Alpha measured 0.737 and 0.757, respectively, showing an excellent internal consistency on the instrument. This study helped me define my final dissertation's scope, research questions, and ambition.

Study Sample

For the qualitative research that provided the impetus for this book, participants were screened based on a set of standard eligibility criteria (e.g., aged 18 or more) and for leadership orientations from the existing questionnaire of the study referenced above (Corbett & Sweeney, 2020). The variable used a Likert five-point scale with a combination of ten items based on Q24 of the original research questionnaire. Items were based on querying respondents about their impressions of leadership. Only individuals who met the inclusion criteria for this study were invited to participate. A qualitative instrument was developed to collect data supporting grounded theory development. It used elements of the aforementioned quantitative study, allowing the instrumentation to be structured ahead of time. Data for this study were collected using individual in-depth interviews with a semistructured interview guide. The data sought to draw on stories recounted by participants, emphasizing the rich tapestry of their life experiences, leadership practices, and associated learning through positive and adverse events. The interview guide aligned with the central research question and the three sub-questions mentioned above and was designed to explore leaders' and followers' integral social relationships and group behaviors in Asia, where little exploration of leadership has been documented.

Qualitative studies are significantly influenced by the sampling decisions made at the start (Miles et al., 2020). Whom a researcher chooses to speak with establishes the boundaries of a study not only via the respondents' choice but also through their social interactions and the contextual environment. There are many sampling strategies available. This study sample used a purposive design rather than random sampling. The selective sample fit the specific characteristics of the population of interest and reflected participants' perceptions related to the studied phenomenon of Connectivist Leadership (Creswell, 2007; Miles et al., 2020; Richards & Morse, 2013). This study's scope included a delineated setting, which was the geographic perimeter commonly defined as the Asia-Pacific (APAC) region. This area consists of 47 countries throughout East and South Asia, Southeast Asia, and Oceania (World Population Review, 2020). Consequently, the study utilized a within-case sampling strategy where the sample was nested in certain countries in Asia. To scope for diversity, the study included participants from markets that were the largest in the area, including China, India, and Indonesia (World Population Review, 2020), and the smallest, such as the city-state of Singapore. This sampling approach also enabled an equal balance within Asian country clusters. This within-case sampling approach was driven by the study's central question, which centered on exploring leadership as a phenomenon in Asia without concern for global representativeness.

The sample was developed through a theoretical sampling strategy, using the emerging analysis to guide the selection of participants upfront. Interpretive research, such as the current study, uses theoretical sampling to guide the selection of respondents and setting based on how well they fit with the phenomenon under review (Onwuegbuzie & Leech, 2007). Grounded theory research is not driven by a concern for representativeness but rather by the central research question and the conceptual framework that supports it. Here, the sampling design was conducted in a multistage procedure to identify clusters of organizations and individuals within them that met the studied phenomenon (Creswell, 2007). The sample was opportunistic and leveraged a snowball sampling approach, allowing salient participants to recommend people they saw as taking part in the phenomenon within a leader–follower collaborative team relationship. They also recommended other participants who demonstrated a similar leadership phenomenon in other workplaces. The final sample was developed from two sources: (1) identified respondents from the earlier quantitative research study (Corbett & Sweeney, 2020) who provided their contact information and expressed the desire to be contacted for future research, and (2) new participants from the convenience sampling based on reputational case selection who met the screening criteria.

The population of interest included companies that presented three fundamental characteristics aligned with the study's conceptual framework. First, companies were culturally located in Asia, allowing an investigation of the relationship between leadership and culture. Second, the companies selected facilitated technologically based knowledge creation, which helped the study evaluate the importance of network-forming processes in leadership enactment. Finally, participating companies practiced collective and connected leadership approaches. Based on the literature review, Chinese firms needed to meet the criteria of modern Chinese leadership (Zhou et al., 2019) to participate in the study. Only private companies that were not government-owned were selected. These firms exhibit very different leadership approaches than those of Chinese state enterprises, which practice traditional forms of leadership anchored in Confucian values, communist ideology, and hierarchy (McDonald, 2012; Rowley & Ulrich, 2012; Zhou et al., 2019). In contrast, this study was interested in an emerging leadership phenomenon, where people are shifting their understanding and practices of leadership from a process led primarily by an individual based on power, authority, control, and hierarchy to a system of shared relationships based on connecting people and information sources to create collective influence.

Respondents were also screened according to their leadership orientations based on a previously validated questionnaire used to establish the Connectivist Leadership phenomenon (Corbett & Sweeney, 2020). To qualify, participants needed to self-select items that fit within the status quo or emerging leadership orientation categories. Participants who chose statements within the traditional leadership orientation were excluded. They also needed to meet a few additional inclusion criteria to take part in the research:

- Be aged 18 years or older.
- Reside full-time in a country within the Asia region.
- Be currently employed (full- or part-time).
- Be employed by a private company (nonstate enterprise).
- Work for a company that has offices in the Asia region that encourages the use of networking technologies in the practice of daily work (such as the internet, intranet, social tools, and instant messaging platforms) and promotes collective ways of working (e.g., agile, teamwork, scrum teams).
- Be a mix of leaders of teams of various sizes (under 10 people, 10–49 people, 50–100 people, and more than 100 people) and people with no direct reports.
- Fit within the status quo or emerging leadership orientation category.
- Have offered consent to participate in the study and met all the screening criteria.

Participants who did not meet these criteria were excluded, along with those who failed or refused to sign the informed consent or were unable to interview during the data collection period. All participant and expert identification was anonymized using numbered pseudonyms (i.e., P1 for the first participant and E1 for the first expert). The final sample included 29 individuals, above the threshold of 20, which is the number typically recommended to develop a well-saturated theory for grounded theory (Creswell, 2007). In grounded theory, data saturation is known as "theoretical saturation" and refers to the point where the main concepts required for the formulation of the theory have been discovered and articulated (Glaser & Strauss, 1967), that is, the point at which added data collection will not add anything new that has not already been observed. Using comparative data analysis, it was determined that the optimal level was 29 participants. This saturation was also objectively demonstrated (Morse, 2015) by following these criteria: (1) clear articulation of the purpose of the study, (2) identifying the study population, and (3) ensuring coding stability (Hennink et al., 2016). Collecting the respondents' most important themes and ideas was essential to reaching saturation through salience, or relevance, rather than complete saturation through sheer volume of information.

In addition to the core study sample of 29 participants, a selection of key global experts in the field was consulted. Thirteen experts, scholars, and practitioners weighed in on the phenomenon studied based on their expertise aligned with the study's conceptual framework. They included (1) experts in digital learning and new knowledge creation, (2) theorists of collective leadership approaches and new organizational models, and (3) authorities in intercultural studies and Asian leadership.

Data Collection

Due to the global COVID-19 pandemic and enforced social distancing restrictions, participant and expert leadership interviews took place via video conference call rather than in person, for one month, in August 2020. This format presented some limitations as I could not observe participants in their natural working environment nor witness the interactions across teams *in situ*; however, this also afforded some advantages. For instance, respondents were more readily available and amenable to participate in the interviews, thanks to the convenience provided by the video experience. It also offered the opportunity to probe into and integrate the various technology platforms (i.e., Skype, Webex, MS Teams, Zoom, Google, BlueJeans) that supported the participants' virtual leadership approaches, placing the researcher at the heart of the phenomenon with an opportunity to directly query and witness the role of technology in leadership distribution. Each interview lasted 60 minutes and was audio and video recorded.

Data Analysis

In grounded theory, data collection is guided by the development of emerging theory. For this study, data were collected using formal semistructured interviews, which were systematically collected, organized, analyzed, and interpreted to form a new leadership theory. The final group of individuals interviewed consisted of 42 people: 29 participants and 13 experts. The sample was nested in the Asia region against two major cultural clusters, Confucian Asia (which includes China and Singapore) and Southern Asia (inclusive of India and Indonesia), as defined by the Global Leadership and Organizational Behaviour Effectiveness (GLOBE) study (House & Javidan, 2004). A total of 15 participants fit within the Confucian Asia cluster: 5 from China and 10 from Singapore. Within Southern Asia, ten participants were recruited: six from India and four from Indonesia. Finally, four non-Asian respondents (expatriates) from Asia were recruited: one from China and Indonesia and two from Singapore, respectively. The sample was evenly balanced to avoid bias, with an almost equal number of females (15) and males (14) and a good representation of ages with an equal balance of participants aged 40–49 years old and 50–59 years old (12 individuals, respectively), some younger participants aged 25–39 years old (4), and 1 person over the age of 60. The sample included an extensive list of various types of organizations and a wide range of industries providing a great diversity of voices from participants in categories ranging from aerospace to advertising, technology, management consulting, computer software, finance, agriculture, media, apparel, design, wellness, personal care, executive recruiting, and real estate.

Figure 0.1 provides an overview of each participant detailing their key demographics (age, race/ethnicity, nationality, and gender), location within the Asia region, employment position, and industry. To maintain confidentiality, each participant was classified under a pseudonym, with a number representing their interview.

The 13 experts interviewed were classified into three groups, aligned to the literature review, and included experts in learning, leadership and organization design, and Asian leadership. Figure 0.2 provides an overview of each expert detailing their key demographics (age, race/ethnicity, nationality, and gender), location, current position, and expertise area. To maintain confidentiality, each expert was classified under a pseudonym, with a number representing their interview order. Many experts who agreed to be interviewed for this study were highly respected voices in their field, including researchers, authors, and academics. They comprised a rich sample from seven markets worldwide, representing nine nationalities and 11 PhDs. These experts provided invaluable additional data that enhanced the study findings through data comparison, validation, and interpretation.

Overview of Participants by Geographic Area

ID	Industry/Category	Position	Location	Gender	Nationality	Race / Ethnicity	Age
Singapore-based Asian Participants (10)							
#4	Aerospace and Defence	Government Affairs, SEA, Pacific & S. Korea	Singapore	Female	Korean	Korean	25-39
#5	Advertising	CEO	Singapore	Female	Filipino	Filipino	40-49
#6	Technology Strategy	Partner, Asia Pacific	Singapore	Female	Singaporean	Singaporean	40-49
#8	Global Management Consulting	Expert Principal, APAC Head of Digital	Singapore	Male	Australian	Chinese	25-39
#10	Management Consulting	Founder & CEO	Singapore	Female	Singaporean	Singaporean	50-59
#14	Marketing Consultancy	Principal	Singapore	Female	Singaporean	Chinese	50-59
#15	Computer Software	General Manager, SEA	Singapore	Female	Malaysian	Chinese	40-49
#19	Global Investment Fund	Director, Public Affairs, Sustainability & Stewardship	Singapore	Female	Singaporean	Chinese	40-49
#22	Agricultural Chemicals	Head of Government Affairs and Sustainability, Asia Pacific	Singapore	Female	Filipino	Filipino	50-59
#27	Trade Association	Assistant Director-General	Singapore	Male	Singaporean	Chinese	40-59
China-based Asian Participants (5)							
#2	Media	Managing Partner, APAC	Shanghai	Female	Taiwan	Chinese	50-59
#11	Apparel	Marketing Leader, APAC	Beijing	Female	Chinese	Chinese	50-59
#16	Technology Services	Chief Digital Officer	Hong Kong	Female	Chinese	Chinese	40-49
#20	Technology Platform	Chief Marketing Officer	Shanghai	Male	Canadian	Chinese	50-59
#26	Private Foundation	Head	Shanghai	Female	British	Chinese	40-49
India-based Asian Participants (6)							
#3	Venture Capital	Advisor/Investor	Mumbai	Male	American	Indian	40-49
#7	Advertising	CEO	Mumbai	Male	Indian	Indian	50-59
#9	Creative Consulting	Consultant	Mumbai	Male	Indian	Indian	50-59
#17	Design Agency	Managing Director	Mumbai	Female	Indian	Indian	40-49
#23	Wellness	Vice President of Marketing	Gurgaon	Female	Indian	Indian	40-49
#24	Advertising	Managing Director	Mumbai	Male	Indian	Indian	50-59
Indonesia-based Asian Participants (4)							
#12	Content Production	CEO	Jakarta	Male	Indonesian	Chinese	40-49
#18	Technology Platform	Country Marketing Head	Jakarta	Male	Dutch	Eurasian	25-39
#28	Personal Care	Chief Growth and Digital Transformation Officer	Jakarta	Female	Indonesian	Indonesian	50-59
#29	Technology Platform	Group Marketing Officer	Jakarta	Male	Indonesian	Indonesian	50-59
Asian-based Non-Asian Participants (4)							
#1	Consulting Practice	Vice Chairman & Chief Strategist	China	Male	British	Caucasian	50-59
#13	Talent Recruiting	CEO	Singapore	Male	British	Caucasian	40-49
#21	Technology Platform	Co-founder & Chief Growth Officer	Jakarta	Male	Polish	Caucasian	25-39
#25	Real Estate Group	Senior Vice President	Singapore	Male	American	African-American	60+

Figure 0.1 Overview of Participants by Geographic Area.

Overview of Experts Interviewed by Area of Expertise Aligned to the Review of Literature

ID	Expertise Area	Position	Location	Gender	Nationality	Race / Ethnicity	Age
Expertise Area: Learning							
#4 PhD.	Connectivism & Leadership	Author and Editor, Leadership Consultant	United Kingdom	Male	British	Caucasian	50-59
#7 PhD.	Networked Learning	Professor and Director of Learning, University of Wollongong	Australia	Male	Dutch	Caucasian	40-49
#10 PhD.	Co-Creator of Connectivism	National Research Council Canada	Canada	Male	Canadian	Caucasian	50-59
Expertise Area: Leadership & Organization Design							
#1 PhD	Global Leadership	Adjunct Professor, National University	USA	Female	American	Sri Lankan	25-39
#6 PhD.	Global Leadership	Adjunct Professor, INSEAD Business School	United Kingdom	Male	Swedish	Caucasian	50-59
#13 PhD.	Global Leadership	Chief Cognitive Officer	Hong Kong	Male	Australian	Caucasian	40-49
#8 M.L.	Organization Design	Angel Investor, Senior Advisor in Asia & Europe	Sweden	Male	German	Caucasian	50-59
#11	Organization Design	Enterprise Coach for Business Agility	Singapore	Female	Australian	Caucasian	40-49
#12 PhD.	Organization Design	President & CEO of Buurtzorg Asia	Hong Kong	Male	German	Caucasian	50-59
Expertise Area: Asia							
#2 PhD.	Asian Consumer Behavior	Professor of Marketing, Singapore Management University (SMU)	Singapore	Male	Singaporean	Indian	40-49
#3 PhD.	Business in Asia	Associate Professor, Management Department at ESSEC School of Business	Singapore	Male	Indian	Indian	40-49
#5 PhD.	Leadership in Asia, Diversity & Inclusion	Author, Leadership Speaker Founder & CEO at The Horan Group	Singapore	Female	American	Caucasian	50-59
#9 PhD.	Asian Consumer Behavior	Deputy Head of Department Associate Professor of Marketing at National University of Singapore (NUS)	Singapore	Female	Singaporean	Chinese	40-49

Figure 0.2 Overview of Experts by Area of Expertise.

The interviewed experts helped identify, develop, and relate concepts from the raw data; gave theoretical meaning to participants' lived experiences; and provided new language for theorizing concepts and their relationships.

Limitations

All studies have their limitations, which the researcher must bear in mind. One of the key characteristics of qualitative data is that it is *made* rather than collected per se (Richards & Morse, 2013). Taking this factor into account, this study built a variety of data sources into its research design to explore the phenomenon from different angles. One limitation is the methodology itself. Although grounded theory is "one of the most sophisticated and developed approaches to rigorous qualitative (non-numerical) research" (Simon & Goes, 2013, p. 104), it does not provide quantitative data to measure or quantify the phenomenon described precisely. Because a convenience sample was used rather than a random sample, the study results do not apply to the general population. The geographic scope presents another limitation. The data were collected among participants based on a large and culturally diverse region, which led to variations across markets and required the researcher to use conjecture until patterns emerged. Another factor of the research is that interviews were conducted in English due to research limitations imposed under regulations of the United States Food and Drug Administration (FDA) and its research Institutional Review Board, formally designated to review and monitor research involving human subjects. The participants' spoken languages can affect the data quality (Cormier, 2018). Thus, it was the researcher's responsibility to see to the data quality and mind the accuracy of the intent of the ideas expressed.

Most importantly, a researcher must attend to their own bias. My cultural background is not Asian. This defining characteristic, along with my European cultural origins and professional experience as a C-suite leader who worked in Asia for over 15 years, may have posed an inadvertent bias to the data collection and interpretation. As an active participant in the research setting, I took note of the following aspects of my positionality: my social constructivist worldview, the use of my professional network for developing the sample of convenience, and my cultural and linguistic positionality in the context of this study with Asian participants.

Language

It is impossible to write a book on leadership without some fundamental concepts that have defined the field of study, including the use of the terms "leader," "follower," followership," and "leadership." While I use this language to establish a common foundation for sharing my ideas, I urge the reader to leave most of their preexisting views at the door. As Rost (1991) explains, diverse phenomena have been studied in the name of leadership, and this book aims to challenge how most of these have been previously conceived.

In this book, I will make use of specific terms that are defined as follows:

- *Leadership*: Is "an influence relationship among leaders and followers who intend real changes that reflect their mutual purposes" (Rost,

1991, p. 102). This study anchors its approach to leadership on this definition, which recognizes leadership through collective influence, multidirectional relationships, and common purpose building aimed at creating positive change.

- *Culture:* Is a complex social phenomenon described as "the collective programming of the mind that distinguishes the members of one group or category of people from others" (Hofstede et al., 2010, p. 6).
- *Connectivism:* Is a learning theory (Downes, 2007; Siemens, 2005) that provides a theoretical framework for understanding learning in a digital age. It asserts that internet technologies (e.g., the World Wide Web, wikis, search engines, social networks, online discussion forums, and artificial intelligence) have radically transformed learning and knowledge into a network-forming process, resulting in new ways of learning and teaching, and a knowledge ecology where learning is organized within a network.
- *Connectivist Leadership:* Describes a new kind of leadership based on the learning theory of connectivism to redefine leadership. "Connectivist Leadership redefines the leadership paradigm for the twenty-first century by recognizing that leadership is a dynamic, connected, and collective influence process, based on the principles of digital knowledge and interpersonal neural networks" (Corbett & Spinello, 2020, p. 8).
- *Heroic leadership*: Is the expression of a traditional leader-centric paradigm where leadership is enacted by a single focal leader who influences others by resorting to authority, power, or coercion. Effective performance is predicated on a single heroic individual with the right skills to motivate others through unidirectional influence (Bradford & Cohen, 1998, Calder, 1977; Meindl et al., 1985).
- *Post-heroic leadership:* Is an alternative paradigm to heroic leadership, which shifts leadership from a focus on individualism to inclusive collective practice and the leadership system (Bradford & Cohen, 1998). Yukl noted, "The leadership actions of any individual leader are much less important than the collective leadership provided by members of the organization" (1999, pp. 292–293).
- *Distributed leadership*: Is a post-heroic leadership perspective that recognizes the influence of teams and shared influence to enact leadership through various approaches, such as collective and shared leadership (Gronn, 2002).
- *Western-centric leadership:* Is the recognition that dominant theories of leadership have been developed by Western thinkers, primarily from North America, introducing underlying cultural biases and assumptions of power and dominance (House & Javidan, 2004; Wilson, 2016).

Structure of the Book

This book is a research-inspired monograph presented in three parts. Part 1 sets the context for the study findings by describing a new geography of leadership. It contends that leadership is now conceived at a new scale of human experience based on three critical factors: (1) localization, (2) Asianification, and (3) the network imperative. Part 2 explains why and how Asia is becoming the leadership sandbox of the future and lays out new leadership ideas and models that are redefining how leadership is practiced, the individuals and teams it involves, and the end goal of leadership. Part 3 details the implications of the research findings, describing the evolving leadership constructs of the last decade and offers new language required to describe the phenomenon at hand. It also proposes a practitioner's starter kit for implementing new leadership practices in organizations and outlines how participants and leading experts predict the future of leadership in years to come. The book ends by encouraging readers to enact the new leadership ideas presented herein and to have the courage to lead in new networked ways.

Leadership Provocations

Almost everything that is touted about leadership comes from Western traditions and literature. Inherent biases have led to prevailing theories of leadership based on power, assumptions of rationality, and a highly individualistic representation of leaders. This book presents a radically new opportunity for leadership based on the voices of Asian leaders and their teams. It articulates a new form of connected and collective leadership, generating shared meaning, purpose, and community-building. Key lessons can be drawn for global leaders, and new pathways can be established for a new era of leadership entirely for, and based on, human connection. Readers are encouraged to suspend their beliefs and explore new ideas on who is involved in the leadership dynamic, how it happens, and its end goals. The book pokes at biases that have standardized the current views of leadership, blurred notions of intercultural competence, and created a discourse of leadership that has institutionalized ideas, behaviors, and language that need reinvention.

Provocation 1: Everyone Is a Leader

To begin, it is imperative to rethink the unit of study of leadership. Leadership conjures images of the one lonely hero, often male, with extraordinary abilities and powers over others; think Spartacus, Gandhi, and Caesar. The conventional wisdom has been that some are born or appointed leaders, and others are de facto followers. Over the years, most books on leadership and research studies have profiled leadership in terms of the influence of a single individual over others. In this dynamic, followers are subordinates, subjugated by an elite who has the power to order them and make decisions based on the vision of one who speaks for the majority. This book aims at "decolonizing leadership" (Schockman et al., 2019, p. xxiv) by recognizing the equal power, rights, and responsibilities of all those involved in leadership. Leadership effectiveness is not a causal chain of variables ignited by a solo vision but a symbiotic relationship based on diversity, collective consciousness, and distributed intelligence. Leadership is not leader-centric but team-centric. Alas, the limitations of language are apparent here as it can be difficult to delineate the perimeter of the "leader" in the totality of what and whom "leader-ship" involves. This book aims to understand and explore all the roles in a leadership network and discard the myth of the heroic leader to "surrender the me for the we," as The National Basketball Association (NBA) coach Phil Jackson urged his superstar (and often egotistical) players. This book focuses on the shared journey of leadership where all participants have collective agency for shared meaning; therefore, it asks readers to be willing to embrace the idea that everyone is a leader. This foundational premise broadens the scope of inquiry into what leadership is today and can become in the future.

Provocation 2: Leadership Manifests a Zeitgeist

Most leadership books base their definitions and explorations on immutable concepts as if leadership could be studied consistently and unshakably across time. This approach is flawed. Leadership reflects the times and has evolved alongside society's ideas about organizations, culture, and life. As noted by Mendenhall et al. (2017, p. 16), leadership is a construct that follows the zeitgeist and is conceived around reciprocal relations, mutual meaning-making, and the interactions of a group. Leadership mirrors civilization, human beliefs, and ways of being and learning. It is critical to acknowledge the greater context in which the research of this book took place as it primed the findings presented. Today's world favors reciprocal relationships, group interactions, real-time social exchanges, and a heavy reliance on networking technology in all facets of life. Despite cultural differences and global inequities, humans live in a networked era, and the understanding of leadership must keep pace with this dramatic change. Recognizing this reality will help readers yield more from this book by understanding what is being presented in the context upfront and possibly anticipate leadership's next inflection points.

Provocation 3: Leadership Requires Emotion

Contrary to what behavioral theories argued at the start of the twentieth century, leadership is not a matter of conditioning, the result of an action–reaction, or a hard science based exclusively on logic and reason. Leadership deals with people and how they relate and come together to achieve extraordinary things. This book emphasizes the relational aspect of leadership and, thus, the significance of emotion. A key finding from this research is how feelings matter to leadership: vulnerability, bonding, empathy, Emotional Intelligence (EQ), compassion, friendship, kinship, and mentoring. All these emotions and feelings are key enablers of outstanding leadership. The findings show a critical inflection point in consciousness on the importance of group dynamics. This is obvious yet rarely documented: without emotion, there is no connectivity, meaning-making, or possible leadership.

Provocation 4: Leadership for Connected Consciousness

By shifting the focus of leadership to collective agency, the end goal of leadership becomes about relationship building rather than control. This book explores leadership for connection, not persuasion or domination. As a result, leadership is constructed not as an efficient or effective process but as a form of human energy and emergence. A key finding from the research is the opportunity to challenge conventionally accepted views on the end goal of leadership. In a management setting, leadership is often proxied through corporate goals. But what leaders and their teams described in this study is that leadership is a connection/network-forming process that uses emotional sensing and attuning to generate collective agency and a greater sense of purpose. The shared meaning far surpasses the corporate goals that may have been at the project's onset and the actors' selection. The actual end game of leadership is the social product that comes from networking and allows everyone to transcend a singular first-person experience into collective intelligence. Psychology professor Carol Dweck argues that there is a theory of incremental intelligence with learning (Dweck & Henderson, 1989). In her research, Dweck expresses the belief that intelligence is malleable and that the brain can continue to form new connections stimulated by new experiences with neuroplasticity. Similarly, this book presents evidence that there is incremental leadership with connectivity. Leadership increases with new connections, which makes the outcome (connected consciousness) far greater than the sum of the parts (the individual leader). Ultimately, connections considerably enhance the experience of everyone in the leadership network.

Why *Leadership on a Blockchain*?

The Essence of Networked Leadership

More than a catchy headline, *Leadership on a Blockchain* captures the essence of what Asia can teach us about networked leadership. The title of this book was directly lifted from the study participants' own words, who described emerging practices in Asia as leadership on a blockchain phenomenon. This metaphor will become apparent in Part 2 of the book, which details why and how Asia is uniquely placed to become the leadership sandbox of the future. Aspects of Asian culture have created a fertile soil for team behaviors and the importance of networks at home and in professional settings. The Chinese call these practices "guanxi," which refers to having strong personal relationships that create moral obligations. These trusted social networks are often life-defining and lasting. Furthermore, Asia's hyper-advanced social networking behaviors, use of mobile technology, and youthful demographics have catapulted the region to the forefront of networked practices in all facets of life.

Leadership on a Blockchain describes how leaders and teams in Asia are shifting their understanding and practices of leadership from a process led primarily by an individual to a system of collective and digitally connected relationships. As a concept and a descriptive account of how leaders and teams operate, it captures the logic of networked information technology to understand how leadership has transformed into a distributed and connected process. Applying blockchain principles (distributed, networked, shared information) to leadership can provide a new perspective on the ontology and reexamining leadership's definition and efficacy. Blockchain has been hailed as a game-changer as it is a peer-to-peer network where no single participant or user controls the exchange. As a result, the power is distributed among all the participants in the network, which results in no single stakeholder being able to manipulate or close the chain of blocks or shut it down. Blockchain applications are virtually limitless as a distributed digital ledger of time-stamped transactions, creating more efficient ways of distributing, securing, and sharing information.

Unsurprisingly, the rise of Web3, social networks, and crowd-based effects have influenced the emergence of new leadership models and decentralized management and organizational governance, such as the advent of DAOs (decentralized autonomous organizations). In the last decade, leadership scholars have been calling for a new focus on nonhierarchical, connected, and collectivist leadership, enabling more horizontal and distributed modes of influence for increased effectiveness through inclusiveness and participation. Hopefully, leadership on a blockchain can result in new ways of naming, visualizing, practicing, and teaching leadership within a unique network ecology.

What does it mean when leadership is on a blockchain, a framework where technology and networks are accounted for? Can leadership be reimagined as a decentralized, transparent, and peer-to-peer process? Can leadership exist in new governance structures that distribute power and decision-making and establish trust as a new business protocol empowering everyone? These pressing questions will be answered in the upcoming sections of this book through the voices of Asian leaders, their team members, and the perspectives of international leadership experts.

Inspiring New Meaning

As new technologies bring us closer together and the internationalization of capital, trade, and people create greater interdependence and competition, it is essential for organizations to attract and grow leaders who can skillfully respond to the opportunities and challenges of a more interconnected and hyper-localized world. According to the Global Leadership Forecast 2018 (International Development Dimensions et al., 2018), which surveyed more than 1,000 C-level executives worldwide on their biggest global concerns, leadership and talent were the top-rated items by 64% of respondents. Leadership is the biggest concern for Chief Executive Officers (CEOs) when it comes to executing their strategy successfully. This worry is ahead of other formidable challenges, such as political instability, global recession, terrorism, and climate change. Of the 2,500 human resources professionals surveyed in the same study, 65% reported that their leaders lacked high-quality, effective development plans (International Development Dimensions et al., 2018). Dr. Evan Sinar, who led the global research study, noted that expectations were rising and that leaders needed to work increasingly collaboratively and demonstrate an understanding of digital technology. He indicated that today's leaders "need to be highly adaptable, hyper-collaborative, and able to leverage data to make better decisions" (Caprino, 2018, para. 3). Research shows not only the primacy of leadership in executing strategy but also the urgency of the topic as significant gaps in leadership training remain. Fully 38% of survey respondents on global human capital rated building leadership as an urgent business issue that must be accelerated (Stephan et al., 2014). Furthermore, "companies see the need for leadership at all levels, in all geographies, and across all functional areas" (Stephan et al., 2014, p. 7).

The findings in this book will aid in building workforce capabilities to broaden, deepen, and accelerate leadership development. New knowledge is required to prepare the next generation of leaders in an increasingly data-led and networked world and provide alternative leadership approaches. A new understanding of leadership will present significant value to business practitioners by

- Providing actionable intelligence to address one of the most pressing business issues of our times – fostering leadership capacity
- Helping organizations position themselves for future success and gain a competitive edge with a set of principles on which their leadership practices can be based
- Addressing the significant readiness gap of organizations to grow and develop leaders, especially those in Asia or planning to work there
- Offering alternative ways to distribute leadership through more collective and digitally connected approaches.

Moreover, I hope that disrupting some of the long-lasting assumptions about leadership will inspire new meaning for those who practice leadership, both as leaders and as team members alike, and help bring a new level of social equity to the leadership field.

References

Bandura, A. (1977). Self-efficacy: Toward a unifying theory of behavioral change. *Psychological Review*, 84(2), 191–215. https://doi.org/10.1037/0033-295X.84.2.191

Barnard, C. I. (1968). *The functions of the executive*. Harvard University Press.

Barth, R. (1988). School: A community of leaders. In A. Lieberman (Ed.), *Building a professional culture in schools* (pp. 129–147). Teachers College Press.

Blunt, P., & Jones, M. L. (1997). Exploring the limits of Western leadership theory in East Asia and Africa. *Personnel Review*, 26(1/2), 6–23. https://doi.org/10.1108/00483489710157760

Bradford, D. L., & Cohen, A. R. (1998). Power Up: Transforming Organizations Through Shared Leadership (1st ed.). John Wiley & Sons, Inc.

Brewster, C., & Bournois, F. (1991). Human resource management: A European perspective. Personnel Review, 20(6), 4–13. https://doi.org/10.1108/EUM0000000000800

Bruner, J. S. (1961). *The process of education*. Harvard University Press.

Calder, B. J. (1977). An attribution theory of leadership. *Journal of Consumer Research*, 4(1), 29–38. https://doi.org/10.1086/208676

Caprino, K. (2018). The changing face of leadership: 10 new research findings all leaders need to understand. *Forbes*. https://www.forbes.com/sites/kathycaprino/2018/02/28/the-changing -face-of-leadership-10-new-research-findings-all-leaders-need-to-understand/#3 a166dde6197

Corbett, F., Fraizer, L., Madjidi, F., & Sweeney, M. (2018). The rise of connectivist leadership. *The IAFOR Research Archive*. http://25qt511nswfi49iayd31ch80-wpengine.netdna-ssl.com/wp-content/uploads/papers/mediasia2018/MediAsia2018_42793.pdf

Corbett, F., & Spinello, E. (2020). Connectivism and leadership: Harnessing a learning theory for the digital age to redefine leadership in the twenty-first century. *Heliyon*, 6(1). https://doi.org/https://doi.org/10.1016/j.heliyon.2020.e03250

Cormier, G. (2018). The language variable in educational research: An exploration of researcher positionality, translation, and interpretation. *International Journal of Research & Method in Education*, *41*(3), 328–341. https://doi.org/10.1080/1743727X.2017.1307335

Creswell, J. W. (2007). Qualitative inquiry & research design: Choosing among five approaches. Sage Publications.

Davis, S. M., & Lawrence, P. R. (1977). *Matrix*. Addison-Wesley Publishing.

De Smet, A., Kleinman, S., & Weerda, K. (2019). *The helix organization*. McKinsey Quarterly. https://www.mckinsey.com/business-functions/organization/our-insights/the-helix-organization

Dewey, J. (1922). *Human nature and conduct*. Holt.

Downes, S. (2007, February). *What connectivism is*. [Blog]. https://www.downes.ca/post/38653

Downes, S. (2008). An introduction to connective knowledge. *Media, knowledge & education: Exploring new spaces, relations, and dynamics in digital media ecologies*. https://www.oapen.org/download?type=document&docid=449459#page=84

Drucker, P. F. (2006). *The practice of management* (1st ed.). Collins.

Dweck, C. S., & Henderson, V. L. (1989). *Theories of Intelligence: Background and Measures*.

Fayol, H. (1916). *General and industrial management*. Pitman Publishing.

Foucault, M. (1972). The archaeology of knowledge and the discourse on language. Tavistock.

Galbraith, J. R. (2016). *The star model*. jaygalbraith.com. https://www.jaygalbraith.com/images /pdfs/StarModel.pdf

Glaser, B., & Strauss, A. (1967). *The discovery of grounded theory*. Aldine.

Gronn, P. (2002). Distributed leadership as a unit of analysis. *The Leadership Quarterly*, *13*(4), 423–451. https://doi.org/10.1016/S1048-9843(02)00120-0

Hennink, M. M., Kaiser, B. N., & Marconi, V. C. (2016). Code saturation versus meaning saturation: How many interviews are enough? *Qualitative Health Research*, 27(4), 1–18. https://doi.org/10.1177/1049732316665344

Hock, D. (2000). *Birth of the chaordic age*. Berrett-Koehler Publisher.

Hofstede, G. (1980). Culture's consequences: International differences in work related values. Sage Publishing.

Hofstede, G., Hofstede, G. J., & Minkov, M. (2010). *Cultures and organizations: Software of the mind, intercultural cooperation and its importance for survival* (3rd ed.). McGraw Hill.

House, R. J., & Javidan, M. (2004). Overview of GLOBE. In R. J. House, P. J. Hanges, M. Javidan, P.W. Dorfman, & V. Gupta (Eds.), *Culture, leadership, and organizations: The GLOBE study of 62 societies* (pp. 9–48). Sage Publications.

International Development Dimensions, The Conference Board, & EYGM. (2018). *The global leadership forecast 2018*. https://www.ddiworld.com/glf2018

Knowles, M., Holton, E., & Swanson, R. (2005a). Andragogy in practice. In M. Knowles, E. Holton, & R. Swanson (Eds.), *The adult learner: The definitive classic in adult education and human resource development* (pp. 138–162). Elsevier.

Köhler, W., & Winter, E. (1925). *The mentality of apes*. Harcourt Brace.

Kreitzer, M. J., Monsen, K. A., Nandram, S., & De Blok, J. (2015). Buurtzorg Nederland: A global model of social innovation, change, and whole-systems healing. *Global Advances in Health and Medicine*. https://doi.org/10.7453/gahmj.2014.030

Laloux, F. (2014). Reinventing organizations: A guide to creating organizations inspired by the next stage of human consciousness (1st ed.). Nelson Parker.

Locke, E. A. (1968). Toward a theory of task motivation and incentives. *Organizational Behavior and Human Performance*, *3*(2), 157–189.

Mann, H. (1853). *A few thoughts for a young man: A lecture delivered before the Boston mercantile library*. Harvard University. https://archive.org/details/afewthoughtsfor 02manngoog/page/n5/mode/2up

Maslow, A. (1943). A theory of human motivation. *Psychological Review, 50*(4), 370–396. https://doi.org/10.1037/h0054346

McDonald, P. (2012). Confucian foundations to leadership: A study of Chinese business leaders across Greater China and South-East Asia. *Asia Pacific Business Review*, *8*(4), 465–487. https://doi.org/10.1080/13602381.2012.693770

Meindl, J. R., Ehrlich, S. B., & Dukerich, J. M. (1985). The romance of leadership. *Administrative Science Quarterly*, *78*, 78–102. https://doi.org/10.2307/2392813

Mendenhall, M. E., Osland, J., Bird, A., Oddou, G. R., Stevens, M. J., Maznevski, M. L., & Stahl, G. K. (2017). *Global Leadership: Research, practice, and development*. Taylor and Francis.

Miles, M., Huberman, M., & Saldaña, J. (2020). *Qualitative data analysis: A methods sourcebook* (4th ed.). Sage Publications.

Mintzberg, H. (1979). *The structuring of organizations*. Prentice-Hall.

Morse, J. (2015). "Data were saturated..." *Qualitative Health Research*, *25*(5), 587–588. https://doi.org/10.1177/1049732315576699

Onwuegbuzie, A., & Leech, N. (2007). A call for qualitative power analysis. *Quality and Quantity*, *41*, 105–121. https://doi.org/10.1007/s11135-005-1098-1

Pavlov, I. (1927). *Conditioned reflexes*. Dover.

Piaget, J. (1952). *The origins of intelligence in children* (2nd ed.). International University Press.

Piaget, J. (1977). The role of action in the development of thinking. In W. F. Overton & J. M. Gallagher (Eds.), *Advances in research and theory* (pp. 17–42). Plenum Press.

Richards, L., & Morse, J. (2013). Readme first for a user'suser's guide to qualitative methods (3rd ed.). Sage.

Robertson, B. J. (2015). Holacracy: The new management system for a rapidly changing world. Henry Holt and Company.

Rost, J. C. (1991). *Leadership for the twenty-first century*. Praeger.

Rowley, C., & Ulrich, D. (2012). Introduction: Setting the scene for leadership in Asia. *Asia Pacific Business Review*, *18*(4), 451–463. https://doi.org/10.1080/13602381.2012.694726

Schein, E. (2017). *Organizational culture and leadership* (5th ed.). Wiley & Sons.

Schockman, E., Hernandez, V., & Boitano, A. (Eds.). (2019). *Peace, reconciliation and social justice leadership in the 21st century: The role of Leaders and Followers*. Emerald Publishing Limited.

Siemens, G. (2005). Connectivism: A learning theory for the digital age. *International Journal of Instructional Technology & Distance Learning*, 2005, 1–9. https://jotamac.typepad.com/jotamacs _weblog/files/Connectivism.pdf

Siemens, G. (2006). *Knowing knowledge*. Lulu.com Books.
Simon, M. K., & Goes, J. (2013). *Dissertation & scholarly research: Recipes for success* (2013 ed.). Dissertation Success.
Skinner, B. F. (1938). *The behavior of organisms*. Macmillan.
Smith, A. (2008). An inquiry into the nature and causes of the wealth of nations: A selected edition (K. Sutherland Ed.). Oxford Paperbacks.
Snow, C. C. (2015). Organization in the age of competition, cooperation, and collaboration. *Journal of Leadership & Organizational Studies*, 22, 433–442.
Stephan, M., Vahdat, H., Walkinshaw, H., & Walsh, B. (2014). *Global human capital trends 2014: Engaging the 21st-century workforce*. https://www2.deloitte.com/content/dam /Deloitte/ar/Documents/human-capital/arg_hc_global-human-capital-trends-2014 _09062014 (1).pdf
Swett, J. (1876). *History of the public school system of California*. Bancroft and Company. https://books.google.com.sg/books?id=DvE4AAAAIAAJ&pg=PA218&redir_esc=y#v=onepage&q&f=false
Taylor, F. W. (1911). *The principles of scientific management*. Harper & Brothers.
Thorndike, E. L. (1913). *Educational psychology*. Teachers College, Columbia University.
Tolman, E. C. (1932). *Purposive behavior in animals and men*. The Century Co.
Trist, E. (1981). *The evolution of socio-technical systems: A conceptual framework and an action research program*. Quality of Working Life Centre.
Ulieru, M., Brennan, R. W., & Walker, S. S. (2002). The holonic enterprise: A model for Internet-enabled global manufacturing supply chain and workflow management. *Integrated Manufacturing Systems*, *13*(8), 538–55. https://doi.org/10.1108/09576060210448125
Vygotsky, L. S., & Cole, M. (1978). Mind in society: The development of higher psychological processes. Harvard University Press.
Watson, J. B. (1930). *Behaviorism*. W.W. Norton.
Weber, M. (1979). *Economy and society: An outline of interpretive sociology*. University of California Press.
Wilson, S. (2013). *Thinking differently about leadership: A critical history of the form and formation of leadership studies*. Massey University. https://www.researchgate.net /publication/265208344_Thinking_differently_about_leadership_A_critical_history_of_the_form_and_formation_of_leadership_studies
Wilson, S. (2016). *Thinking differently about leadership: A critical history of leadership studies*. Edward Elgar.
World Population Review. (2020). APAC Countries | Asia-Pacific Countries 2020. *World Population Review*. http://worldpopulationreview.com/countries/apac-countries/
Yukl, G. (1999). An evaluation of conceptual weaknesses in transformational and charismatic leadership theories. *Leadership Quarterly*, *10*(2), 285–305. https://doi.org/10.1016/S1048-9843(99)00013-2
Zhou, Y., Kim, S., & Ru, D. (2019). Chivalrous idealist and pragmatic strategist: The influence of Mohist values on Ma Yun'sYun's leadership in China. *Asia Pacific Business Review*, *5*(2), 273–287. https://doi.org/10.1080/13602381.2018.1548546

Part I

A New Geography of Leadership

Part I

Introduction

Introduction

Tim Marshall (2015) proclaimed that we are all prisoners of geography as it shapes our history and destiny. This twentieth-century environmental determinist approach emphasizes the critical role that geography (i.e., climate, topography, oceans) plays in socioeconomic development and leadership. Today, leadership's borders are defined less by physical boundaries than by cultural, economic, and technological forces impacting how we interact and connect with others. "The nature of geopolitical competition is evolving from war over territory to war over connectivity," said Khanna (2016), explaining that connectivity, more so than geography, now predicates our destiny.

This part examines the new geography of leadership drawn from a shifting ideology about the world, the rise of Asia as a new global power, and the network imperative changing international organizations, business models, and learning across the globe.

References

Khanna, P. (2016). *Connectography: Mapping the future of global civilization*. Random House.

Marshall, T. (2015). *Prisoners of geography: Ten maps that explain everything about the world*. Scribner.

DOI: 10.4324/9781003399377-3

1 A Shifting Leadership Ideology

Abbreviated History of Leadership Theories

Leadership is always a reflection of a moment in time and the central tenets of civilization. According to Yukl (2013), five significant milestones have marked the evolution of leadership theory: (1) the trait approach from 1900 to the 1940s, (2) the behavioral approach in the 1950s, (3) the situational approach from the 1960s to the 1970s, (4) the power–influence approach from the 1980s to the 1990s, and (5) the integrative approach with contemporaries. Without oversimplifying 100 years of leadership history, it is possible to broadly categorize key leadership moments into a few endeavors and approaches (see Figure 1.1):

- A focus on being – Great man/trait leadership theories, which assume that leadership is based on power and domination
- A focus on doing – Transactional leadership theories, which operate on the principle of "stimulus–response" and directive patterns of behavior
- A focus on thinking – Contingency/situational leadership theories, which leverage mental activity to determine the right circumstances for action
- A focus on feeling – Relational leadership theories (path–goal, servant, transformational, and ethical) focused on relationships and emotional affect
- A focus on connecting – Networked leadership theories (team leadership, shared leadership, distributed leadership), embracing a view of a hyperconnected world with systems thinking and sense-making.

Being

Safferstone (2005) notes that before the 1930s, much of what was known about leadership was pieced together from the Bible (D. Evans, 2019), Sun

DOI: 10.4324/9781003399377-4

Leadership Theories: Significant Historical Milestones

Leadership Theories	Theorists	
Being		
Great Man Theory - "In born" leadership	Carlyle (1841)	Dominating
Trait Theory - Good leaders are great men, heroes, and unique individuals who have natural attributes such as superior intellect, and heroic courage	Kohs & Irle, (1920) Bernard (1926) R.D. Mann (1959)	
Doing		
Skill-based Leadership - Leadership as a set of supervisory administrative skills	Katz (1955)	Directive
Style-based Leadership - Leadership behavior is based on structure (production orientation) and consideration (employee orientation)	The Ohio Studies (1957) The Michigan Studies (1966)	
The Leadership Grid - Leadership behavior is based on concern for production and people	Blake & Mouton (1964), Bass (1985)	
Thinking		
Situational Leadership - Leadership through the categorization of styles and situations	Hersey & Blanchard (1969)	Situational
Contingency Leadership - Leadership is contingent on the people and context	Stogdill (1948) Fiedler (1964)	
Path-Goal Theory - Leadership through follower satisfaction and motivation and setting	Evans (1970) House (1971)	
Feeling		
Leader-Member Exchange (LMX) - Leadership is based on the interactions between leaders and followers	Dansereau, et al. (1975) Downton (1973)	Relational
Transformational Leadership - Leadership aims to satisfy follower needs by inspiring and engaging them	Burns (1978) Bass (1985)	
Servant Leadership - Leadership consists in serving and driving positive change for others	Greenleaf (1970)	
Authentic Leadership - Leadership gains a moral high ground and is concerned with trust, honesty and good	Avolio (1999) Eagly (2005)	
Ethical Leadership - Promotion of an internalized moral perspective	Brown et al. (2005)	
Spiritual Leadership - Leadership through a calling via vision and values	Fry (2003) P. Palmer (2004)	
Connecting		
Shared/Distributed/Team Leadership - Team-centric leadership based on leader-team interactions	Pearce & Conger (2003)	Networked
Complexity leadership - Focuses on enabling the learning, creative, and adaptive capacity of knowledge-producing organizations	Day et al. (2004) Uhl-Bien et al. (2007)	
e-leadership - Distributed leadership that is mediated by and expressed through technology	Zigurs (2003) Zaccaro & Bader (2003)	
Swarm Leadership - Leadership through networks with distributed knowledge, agency, and decision-making	Gloor (2017) Kelly (2019)	

Figure 1.1 Abbreviated History of Leadership Theories.

Tzu's *The Art of War* dating back from the fifth century BC (Pardo, 2017), Machiavelli's *The Prince* written in the sixteenth century (Worthy & Quinn, 2017), and Clausewitz's *On War* written in the early 1800s (Strachan & Herberg-Rothe, 2008). As these titles suggest, leadership was conceived in relation to conflict and primarily described as the ability to exert power and domination over others. At the turn of the century, the study of leadership formalized with the "Great Man" theory (Carlyle, 1841), based on the assumption that leaders were born, not made, and that leadership traits were genetic and predisposed. Carlyle (1841) continued the set of beliefs promoted by Aristotle in politics, who argued that "from the moment of their birth, some are marked for subjugation and others for command" (Kelly, 2019, p. 12). This leadership approach was also known as the "trait" theory (Bernard, 1926; Kohs & Irle, 1920; Mann, 1959) and highlighted inherited traits, such as intellectual acumen, decisiveness, and personality (Judge & Bono, 2000). Leaders were treated as special people with positional power and considered imbued with superior qualities. Followers were expected to demonstrate their complete obedience to leaders and cooperation. Numerous research studies were conducted to validate in-born and trait leadership theories, but none were conclusive. The study of the "Great Man" theory was largely abandoned from the 1950s onward, primarily due to a lack of supporting evidence. Still, it has remained an underlying assumption in today's practice and the heroic depiction of leaders.

Doing

In the 1950s, leadership took on a more directive approach as "doing" versus "being" (see Figure 1.1). The role of the leader was to exert a set of skills to be an effective administrator, as per Robert Katz's skill-based model of leadership (1955). The goal was to shape others to match organizational goals by performing behavior checks and guiding the hands-on practice of followers, conditioned for immediate feedback and response. As a result, leaders and followers were in a transactional dynamic. Lambert (2002, p. 5) noted that "leadership was not an innate quality, but a behavioral transaction between leader and follower." Behaviorist research guided leadership development by applying behavioral compliance and programmatic conditioning to leadership training, particularly in the US military. Leadership was akin to a learning "treatment" that could be administered and measured with behavioral objectives.

Two landmark research studies known as the Ohio and Michigan studies (Bowers & Seashore, 1966; Hemphill & Coons, 1957) supported the transactional leadership theory by isolating the impact of default leadership styles on behavioral outcomes. These leadership studies determined that effective leadership behaviors were based on task-oriented behaviors and human-oriented behaviors linked to group activity (Bass, 1990). Meanwhile, Michigan studies isolated "employee orientation" and "production orientation" as two main leadership behaviors. Understanding the configuration of these two variables opened the field of leadership studies, which started to examine leadership beyond the inner boundaries of the individual (i.e., Trait theory) and consider the broader external environment in which leadership was enacted. Transactional leadership (Bass, 1985), in contrast with transformational leadership (Burns, 1978), studied how leaders and followers interacted in a structured and rules-based performance environment focused on supervision and tasks.

Thinking

Situational leadership theory, introduced initially in 1969 and updated in 1977, taught the importance of situations on leadership outcomes (Hersey & Blanchard, 1969). This theory assumed that there was no absolute best leadership style; instead, it should be based on "thinking" and adapting to the situation (see Figure 1.1). Leaders were encouraged to adjust how they behaved and supported followers based on assessing two variables: task behavior and relationship behavior. Effective leaders were asked to adapt their leadership – telling, selling, anticipating, or delegating – according to the task's complexity and the follower's readiness. Contingency theory introduced the importance of recognizing the interaction between people and their context (leadership as determined by both the leader and the situation).

A prominent theory in the situational movement was Fiedler's contingency (1964) theory, which introduced three mediating aspects regarding how a leader can take control of a situation: (1) the way followers feel toward their leader, (2) followers' understanding of their tasks, and (3) the degree of power the leader has toward their followers. Central to this strategy was the leader's need to find the situational "favorability" to match their leadership style to the context. New research also presented leadership as a skill and examined it as an activity on a spectrum ranging from employee-centered to production-centered (Katz et al., 1987). This approach was known as the "path–goal theory" of leader effectiveness from the works of M. G. Evans (1970, 1996) and House (1971). The major components of the path–goal theory included four leader behaviors: directive, supportive, participative, and achievement-oriented. Situational, contingency and path–goal leadership theories offered more structure and "predictive power" (Northouse, 2013, p. 127) on leadership effectiveness, and these frameworks have continued to be popularized well into the

1980s and 1990s (Argyris, 1990; McChesney et al., 2012; Senge, 2006) as leadership construction has taken on a more reflective and relational dimension over time.

Feeling

In the 1970s, the study of leadership evolved beyond trait, behavioral, situational, contingency, and path–goal theory to address the broader social aspects of leadership and the feelings in the leadership dynamic (see Figure 1.1). There was a "greater emphasis on social context and interaction that highlighted the importance of followership and produced a generation of relational leaders" (Kelly, 2019, p. 9). From World War II into the 1960s, much of the leadership literature emphasized the leader–follower relationship with a concern for sharing power and influence. The relational leadership scholars proposed a more balanced and equal view of leadership between leaders and followers, which considered leadership a dynamic interaction system (Bolden et al., 2008). From there, the study of leadership became more complex, recognizing the multifaceted interactions between leaders and followers and the need to empower followers through rewards and recognition.

The leader-member exchange (LMX) leadership theory conceptualized leadership "as a process that is centered on the interactions between leaders and followers" (Northouse, 2013, p. 161). This theory recognized that the relationships between leaders and followers were constantly changing. This was a fundamentally different view from leadership theories developed based on traits, styles, or behaviors. LMX theory argued that "the quality of the relationship that develops between a leader and a follower is predictive of outcomes at the individual, group, and organizational levels of analysis" (Gerstner & Day, 1997, p. 827). Early studies of LMX theory from Dansereau et al. (1975) explored the nature of linkages across leaders and followers based on their dyadic relationship, vertical dyads with subordinates, and in-group and out-group relationships. Subsequent LMX studies demonstrated that organizational performance and effectiveness were proportionally related to the nature of the exchange between leaders and members (Graen & Uhl-Bien, 1995). Today, scholarly interest in LMX research remains high as a theory that directs attention to the relational aspect of leadership and the quality of the leader and follower exchange (Anand et al., 2011), indicating its positive contribution and continued relevance to the field of leadership.

The contemporary leadership literature has continued to investigate the affective elements of leadership and the critical role that followers play in the leadership exchange. The original idea of "transformational leadership" (Downton, 1973) was expanded by James Macgregor Burns, who described leaders as "people who tap the motives of followers to reach the goals of leaders and followers better" (1978, p. 18). Burns (1978) distinguished transactional leadership from transformational leadership, aimed at creating a deep connection between the leader and the follower, resulting in increased motivation and mutual empowerment. According to Bass (1985, p. 154), the latter depended highly on the context where the interaction between leaders and followers occurred. Transformational leadership "is more likely to reflect social values and to emerge in times of distress and change, while transactional leadership is more likely to be observed in a well-ordered society."

Overall, only leadership that "is a process that changes and transforms people" can genuinely be called "transformational" (Northouse, 2013, p. 185). It leverages emotions, values, and followers' motives to help them achieve their fullest potential (Avolio, 1999). Leaders seek to empower and nurture followers through strong ideals and visions. To distinguish transformative leaders who have exploitive intentions from genuine and selfless leaders, Bass (1998) created a category of leaders called "pseudotransformational." Power-oriented leaders with low morality were contrasted with those who practiced "authentic transformational leadership" concerned with the common good. This distinction helped introduce an ethical dimension to leadership, later expanded with other forthcoming leadership theories. With a large body of evidence and research, transformational leadership has garnered considerable appeal and is regarded among scholars as one of the most effective contemporary leadership approaches of our times (Antonakis, 2012; Bass & Riggio, 2006; Lowe & Gardner, 2001).

New leadership theories have continued to build on generating followers' trust, engagement, motivation, and empowerment. A theory offering a unique perspective was servant leadership by Greenleaf (1970). Contrary to most leadership theories, which were overly concerned with the leader, this theory primarily focused on followers concerned for their well-being, needs, and capacity development. According to Greenleaf (1970, p. 15), servant leadership "begins with the natural feeling that one wants to serve, to serve first. Then conscious choice brings one to aspire to lead." By reversing the leadership focus, this theory brought leadership into new areas previously unexplored by other theories. It required leaders to place the needs of followers first, shift power and authority to subordinates, provide follower development, act with moral behavior, demonstrate social responsibility within the community at large, and seek to address injustices (Greenleaf, 1970). The ten characteristics of servant leadership are summarized by Spears (2002) as follows: (1) listening, (2) empathy, (3) healing, (4) awareness, (5) persuasion, (6) conceptualization, (7) foresight, (8) stewardship, (9) commitment to the growth of people, and (10) building community. As evidenced by these normative principles, servant leadership was as much a guiding philosophy as a leadership theory. The seminal work of Greenleaf (1970) offered a moralistic philosophical framework, which has become the basis for much of the recent leadership literature.

One significant legacy from the work of Greenleaf is the possibility of grooming a new generation of leaders who can be "healthier, wiser, freer, more autonomous and more likely to become servants themselves" (Barbuto & Wheeler, 2006, p. 321). From the 1990s onward, leadership scholars turned to the development of moral grounding in leaders. The literature integrated the issues of trust, honesty, and ethics within the conceptualization of leadership. Authentic leadership explored how leadership was morally uplifting to followers, as also identified in transformational leadership (Luthans & Avolio, 2003; Zhu et al., 2011). Avolio et al. (2009, p. 423) noted that authentic leadership offered "a pattern of transparent and ethical leader behavior that encourages openness in sharing information needed to make decisions while accepting followers' inputs."

One of the factors isolated as a component of authentic leadership was the leader's introspection, ability to self-regulate and reflect on choices and behaviors, and sense of morality. This criterion enabled another form of leadership considered "ethical" (Brown et al., 2005), described as "the demonstration of normatively appropriate conduct through personal actions and interpersonal relationships, and the promotion of such conduct to followers" (Avolio et al., 2009, p. 424). Avolio's research (1999) showed that ethical leadership was significantly related to organizational performance in employee fulfillment, commitment, performance, and citizenship behavior.

Scholars also explored spiritual leadership (Fry, 2003; Palmer, 2004), defined as "awareness within individuals of a sense of connectedness that exists with their inner selves and the world" (Jamaludin et al., 2011, p. 78). Spiritual leadership aims to create a calling in oneself and others through vision and values to foster higher levels of commitment through a sense of membership. Spiritual leaders extended the practice of transformational leadership with altruistic values such as love and wholeness (Fernando et al., 2009). While some scholars have argued that spiritual leadership should constitute a new leadership paradigm (Dent et al., 2005), it is empirically difficult to train for and measure this approach, which is highly subjective and personal.

Connecting

While leadership constructs based on morality, spirituality, ethics, and well-being remain relevant in the contemporary literature, new forms of leadership based on more participative and networked models have emerged coinciding with the advent of the digital age (see Figure 1.1).

In a content analysis, Corbett et al. (2018) established that the leadership literature experienced a significant change in 2015, with a marked decline from its steady increase since the start of the century. In contrast, search terms for "collective leadership" grew, with network theory characteristics, including transparency, collaboration, teamwork, and distributed decision-making (Corbett et al., 2018). These theories advance more complex views of leadership, challenging the underlying assumptions of the previously reviewed literature, which underline much of what is taught and practiced in the field of leadership studies to date. In these newer leadership paradigms, leadership is no longer defined based on the leader's idealized influence (i.e., dominating, directive, charismatic) or as the result of an exchange between the leader and the follower (i.e., situational, relational) but as an outcome in terms of knowledge creation through a dynamic and collective effort, and ultimately a shared collective state of connectivity.

Different leadership theories have explored shared forms of leadership, where leadership is team-centric based on leader–team interactions (Zaccaro et al., 2009). Leadership genres alternate between "team leadership" (Day et al., 2004; Kogler Hill, 2013), "shared leadership" (Pearce & Conger, 2003; Pearce et al., 2009), and "distributed leadership." These models present similar ideals on how leaders and followers work together in teams. The review of research, however, shows that team leadership is sometimes still described within the traditional views of the leader as a decision-maker directing team decisions. In contrast, some models are more progressive in their views of leadership as a network effect, outcome, and group knowledge creation.

The Hill Model for Team Leadership (Kogler Hill, 2013, p. 291) describes team leadership based on a functional process, which includes leadership decisions, actions, and markers of team effectiveness. This approach remains traditional in its leadership perspective as the leader retains all the vital decisions of the team, setting goals and direction, being responsible for the team's functioning, and selecting the appropriate behaviors for group effectiveness. While the work occurs within a team, leadership interventions remain up to the leader, and not a fully distributed leadership approach. There is no network effect in this way of leading teams.

Shared leadership (Pearce & Conger, 2003, p. 1) defines leadership as "a dynamic, interactive influence process among individuals in groups for which the objective is to lead one another to the achievement of group or organizational goals or both." It sees leadership as a process of reciprocal influence (Carson et al., 2007). Shared leadership recasts leadership into the collective, with distributed individuals collectively leading each other. According to Carson et al. (2007), certain conditions are predictors of shared leadership, including having a shared purpose, giving a voice to all team members, providing external coaching, and extending emotional and psychological support to each other. In their exploration of team leadership, Day et al. (2004) go a step further by characterizing team leadership not just as a process but as a work product from teamwork and learning, which generates an "emergent team property" or state. This perspective seeks to conceptualize team leadership beyond a mere process or outcome, but rather as a unique property of the collective.

Several emergent leadership theories propose examining leadership as a responsive and networked influence model through shared connections and leadership. Goldie (2016, p. 1064) notes that in the field of learning, "there is unlikely to be a single theory that will explain learning in technological enabled networks."

Complexity leadership theory argues that leadership is more than a production activity and encompasses learning, knowledge, creativity, and innovation (Uhl-Bien & Marion, 2008). The theory emphasizes the conditions in which change occurs to facilitate collaborative knowledge. As a leadership theory, it proposes "a leadership paradigm that focuses on enabling the learning, creative, and adaptive capacity of complex adaptive systems (CAS) within a context of knowledge-producing organizations" (Uhl-Bien et al., 2007, p. 298). Complexity theory sees leadership as a collective process, which dynamically brings together random agents in networks to produce knowledge. As a result, leadership can be described as "an emergent phenomenon within complex systems" (Hazy et al., 2007, p. 2).

As more businesses operate internationally and teams interact far from each other, virtual leadership, or e-leadership, proposes to examine leadership that is mediated by and expressed through technology. Zigurs (2003) argues that leadership in the electronic age fundamentally differs from traditional leadership, which uses face-to-face interactions. With virtual teams which experience high levels of autonomy and little direct control due to their geographic, temporal, cultural, and organizational dispersion, leadership must be conceived as "a total system" (Zigurs, 2003). Leadership is no longer enacted by a single individual but distributed across the team as a collective product, with leadership roles rotating as needed. A distinct quality of e-leadership is how technology enables collaborative activities with features that facilitate online brainstorming, document sharing, commenting, voting, and ranking, allowing the distribution of leadership across the entire team and the company. As a result, "leadership in virtual teams is expressed through technology" (Zigurs, 2003, p. 347) rather than merely using it as a tool. Comparing virtual teams to others, Zaccaro and Bader (2003) argue that e-teams have a more significant potential for generating "social capital." They benefit from the broader relationships and networks they operate and the diversity of talents they can recruit.

Another new direction for leadership has been to study the patterns of nature and the biological functions of basic organisms, such as insects, that operate in swarms. As human activity increasingly occurs in social networks, scholars have been keen to construct new leadership models on the metaphor of living species (e.g., bees) to understand the influence of groups, participatory information sharing, cooperative relationships, knowledge sharing, and creation. As humans adjust to learning, working, and playing on social networks, leadership needs to become a "unified living system" that facilitates generative human behaviors based on the power of collaboration (Haywood Rolling, 2013). Extracting decision-making characteristics from swarm behavior, Haywood Rolling (2013, p. 59) has defined principles of swarm intelligence that he argues can shape future leadership practices such as the following:

- Self-organization
- Dispersed control
- Decentralized problem-solving
- The multiplicity of connections across agents
- Diversity of knowledge.

Building on the same swarm leadership concept, Massachusetts Institute of Technology (MIT) researcher Peter Gloor (2017, p. 2) affirms that "the future of business is swarm business" and that leadership is about creating a working swarm. To create a swarm, team members need to follow a five-layer model of collaboration (Gloor, 2017, p. 11), including (1) the physical layer (teamwork), (2) the network layer (technology tools), (3) the signal layer (goal setting), (4) the ethical layer (moral and ethical standards), and (5) the collaboration layer (transparency, fairness, honesty, forgiveness, and listening). In the collaborative, connected future, leadership is a swarm with built-in group responsibility. Using the emerging field of quantum social sciences, Gloor (2017) redefines leadership as a phenomenon that is far deeper than just peer influence or collaboration; he asserts that higher consciousness inherently connects humans and that together they can achieve shared knowledge, behaviors, and wisdom in total synchronicity.

Gloor (2017) outlines four principles that must be followed to build a collective consciousness: (1) empathy, (2) entanglement, (3) reflection, and (4) refocus. Together, these operating principles provide the framework for building collaborative innovation networks (COINs), where self-organizing groups can cooperate over the internet as creators and connectors. In this model, the business structure, traditionally known as a "physical company", becomes a network or COIN, with new laws of ethics and collaborative practices. This perspective opens radically new approaches to understanding human interactions and the possibility of collective intelligence over distance and time.

Bohm discussed the concept of collective knowing and human interconnectedness as part of his exploration of holism, the collective phenomena, and interest in quantum physics (Bohm, 2002). He introduced the concept of the "implicate order" to describe an inner language across humans, an imperceptible level of reality that enfolds humankind into universal consciousness and essential interdependence (Bohm, 2002). Bohm's dialogue model, where he explores the "group mind" (Bohm, 2004), greatly informed Senge's leadership works on collective thinking and work teams as a fundamental unit of the learning organization (2006). The work of Bohm has also been influential in the leadership thinking of Jaworski (2012, p. 24), who opined that "leaders have to develop a new cognitive capability – the capacity to sense and actualize emerging futures. This capacity constitutes a new form of knowledge creation."

In summary, this brief historical examination of leadership theory helps demonstrate the evolution of leadership ideas throughout time. Leadership does not exist in a vacuum; it must be understood as a social, emotional, and cultural construct containing subjective ideas about our time and humanity. Scholars are definitive about the need to change our understanding of leadership in the emerging digital paradigm. According to Jonassen and Land (2012, p. viii), "we have entered a new age" with three significant areas of transformation in thinking: (1) social and affective practice, (2) meaning-making, and (3) collective social dialog.

Trend Lines Affecting Contemporary Leadership Ideology

A key force affecting how leadership is conceived and practiced today is a radical shift in how we look at the scale of our world and make sense of our human experience. Critical thinking on world dynamics has dramatically shifted in the last decade, arising from anti-globalization, political fragmentation, radicalization, and isolationism accelerated by the global pandemic and subsequent widespread border closures. Leadership now sits in an age of democratic erosion, with capitalism under scrutiny, the rise of nationalism and populism, and the decline of multilateral governance norm setting.

Anti-globalization

In the early 2000s, globalization was regarded as a galvanizing force, fostering the interaction and integration of people, companies, economies, and governments worldwide at an unprecedented scale. We wanted and believed in a singular world that could function as one; therefore, leadership opportunities arose from a globalist ideology with world citizens living in civic globalism, thinking and leading globally against the backdrop of international trade and the growing flow of ideas, people, and culture uniting all of humankind (Goldsmith et al., 2003). Much of the leadership literature concerned itself with "global leadership" and the search for a one-size-fits-all model. The field of global leadership development burgeoned with scholars (Bird & Mendenhall, 2016; Mendenhall et al., 2017; Suutari, 2002) responding to the need for universal frameworks and approaches guiding global talent management. In the last decade, however, the world has shifted from theorists of globalization, who described a single global political economy to jointly manage the flow of people, capital, and trade based on US capitalism, to rejecters of a dominant empire and consensus structure (Cox, 2018). Anti-globalization movements have denounced the downside of global governance institutions highlighting their bureaucratic incompetence, mixed record, and ambiguous interests. According to Pankaj Ghemawat (2018), an acclaimed economist in the study of globalization, the retreat of globalization started with the global financial crisis of 2008. It receded further after 2015 with negative news stories questioning the benefits of international trade.

More fundamentally, today's anti-globalist movement aims to challenge globalization's geographic and economic concerns anchored primarily in location and trade to respond to where humans are in the world and ask more deeply about our identity and moral responsibility. In addressing the philosophical aspects of globalization in a more synchronized world, Sloterdijk (2018) encouraged reflection on the sociopsychological consequences of globalization. From this standpoint, globalization can be viewed as a crisis of consciousness about transforming human identity. Historically, human identity has been defined on a national scale through fixed borders, monoculture, and language. More recently, it was reimagined as a unified (and somewhat idealistic) global idea. Today, however, the world is more fragmented, multicultural, and multilingual and needs to embrace a pluralistic future and diverse leadership directions.

The rejection of globalization exposes the necessary reformatting of human thinking and the need to develop an understanding of our interdependence as a species, with new social formations shifting from individual strategies to collective ones for a sustainable future (Trevenna et al., 2018) and new models of networked leadership. Accordingly, there is an undercurrent of anti-globalization in today's leadership ideology as much as there is on the economic and trade relations front. Much of today's leadership concerns are about representing the true diversity of cultures and practices. This affords a considerable opportunity for leadership to move out of the global aspect of leadership anchored heavily in Western leadership paradigms. Leadership can evolve from an ethnocentric set of common standards to being about human interdependence, equality, respect, diversity, and better ways to connect and collaborate in a multicultural world.

Democratic Erosion

Winston Churchill famously said that "democracy is the worst form of government, except for all those other forms that have been tried from time to time" (Churchill, 1947). After the Cold War, democracy, a form of government that gives ordinary citizens the means to rule through free political association, expression, and participation, became the leading political system worldwide. Scholars argued that Western democracy could be the long-lasting answer for collective self-determination. In this regard, political scientist and economist Francis Fukuyama talked of the "triumph of the West, of the Western *idea*" (Fukuyama, 1989). They argued that free-market capitalism and the worldwide spread of liberal democracies were signs of humanity's sociocultural evolution and that they would become a final form of human government (Fukuyama, 1992). In 2011, however, Fukuyama revised his historical outlook, indicating that the American model had become polarizing and ideologically rigid (Fukuyama, 2011b). In the wake of successful non-Western forms of government, he called the US democracy a "vetocracy" (i.e., a dysfunctional system of governance) with the growing influence of special interest groups creating an alternative form of governance (Fukuyama, 2011a).

Further evidence suggests that, lately, "the broad trend toward democracy has stalled and even reversed" (Straus & Driscoll, 2019, p. 184), with many countries around the world embracing authoritarian regimes (e.g., Russia), while others are settling for hybrid political approaches combining elements of authoritarianism and democracy. According to Freedom House, an algorithm that tracks political rights and civil liberties worldwide, while the 1970s saw a gradual trend in democratization, democracies started to stabilize in the 2000s. In 2015, the number of states that were not free increased significantly (Freedom House, 2019). Data on freedom in the world in 2018 revealed that democracy is in a state of crisis, with 37% of the world population not being free and 24% only partially free (Freedom House, 2019). "Seventy-one countries suffered net declines in political rights and civil liberties, with only 35 registering gains. This marked the 12th consecutive year of decline in global freedom" (Freedom House, 2019, para. 2). Many reasons are provided for this democratic retreat, including the anti-globalization movement, increased economic hardships, rising inequality, and widespread political corruption alienating citizens who turned to more assertive regimes in search of order. Political science and sociology professor Larry Diamond noted that democracy had lost its shine worldwide, allowing a dramatic shift in power and behavior (CQ Researcher, 2018).

Democratic erosion exerts a significant force on leadership ideology, and "with widespread democratic backsliding globally, people's support for democracy-eroding leaders is receiving overdue attention" (Simonovitz et al., 2021, p. 1806). The recent surge of heroic leaders in political life, ruling by partisanship, fear, and information control, and populist movements around the world present an alarming context and reverse role modeling for leadership at large. At the same time, these dynamics raise an urgent need for businesses to step into civic life and play a counterbalancing role in addressing leadership erosion. According to the 2022 Edelman Trust Barometer (Edelman, 2022), 61% of respondents globally said that businesses were the most trusted institutions, ahead of non-governmental organization (NGOs) (59%), government (52%), and the media (50%). While corporates outscored government by 53 points on competency, businesses were also 26 points ahead on ethics, resulting in experts saying that "societal leadership is now a core function of business" (Edelman, 2022, p. 1).

Capitalism Under Scrutiny

There is no disputing that today's model of capitalist democracy has come under growing scrutiny. Scholars highlight a state of crisis in the West, characterized by political decay and dysfunction, owing to national corruption, growing global economic inequalities, and a divergence of economic philosophies. The working class has suffered a decline in living standards and joblessness, while political leaders have prescribed policies that, intentionally or not, enriched the elite, undermining faith in capitalism. According to the Organisation for Economic Co-operation and Development (OECD, 2009), regardless of countries' various trends and patterns, economic inequalities have risen everywhere worldwide since the 1980s.

While top-income disparities in Japan, France, and Germany have also drawn public attention, none have experienced such a polarizing share of difference as those in the United States, which has been the beacon of capitalism around the world and driven the emergent post-US economic order after World War II. In the United States, the share of income from the top 1% more than doubled during the last 30 years (Alvaredo et al., 2013). According to Raghuram Rajan, the International Monetary Fund Chief Economist, 58% of all income in the United States was held by the top 1% of the population in 2009 (Rajan, 2010). Marc Benioff, the chairman and co-CEO (Chief Executive Officer) of Salesforce, wrote an opinion piece in *The New York Times*, stating that the current system had engendered "horrifying inequality" and called for urgent action to build a new kind of capitalism, "more fair, equal and sustainable" (Benioff, 2019). Bernie Sanders, an American political activist who served as a US Senator from Vermont, also recently issued an opinion piece in *The Guardian* (Sanders, 2022). He laments that the most important economic and political issues facing the United States were the extraordinary levels of income and wealth inequality due to capitalist greed. In 2022, three multibillionaires (Elon Musk, Jeff Bezos, and Richard Branson) owned more wealth than the bottom half of American society – 160 million Americans. Today, 45% of all new income goes to the top 1%, and CEOs of large corporations make a record-breaking 350 times what their workers earn" (Sanders, 2022, para 2).

Economic inequalities rate highly on the agenda of sociologists because they are proven to have significant consequences on the erosion of social cohesion in society. Inequalities spur political upheaval and conflicts, increase crime rates, and diminish solidarity across groups in society (Werfhorst & Salverda, 2012). The discontent with the capitalist model across the globe has been driven by an alienated middle class left behind while top-income earners profited from favorable tax policy, capital income, and private wealth. The uncertainty toward the Western model of capitalist democracy is having major consequences on leadership at large; it is creating a climate of angst where people are searching for greater equity and rejecting uneven power dynamics to achieve social and economic fairness.

Regionalization and Localization

While democracies are under stress and capitalism is scrutinized, the world is further fragmenting through regionalization and localization. Regional governance has become a new counterforce, with regions acquiring more autonomy, authority, and influence on the world stage (Herz, 2018), creating cooperation at an economic and social level with independent states. Inter-regional trade, capital investment, and culture have resulted in the creation of regional identities, such as "pan-Arabism" and "pan-Africanism" (Herz, 2018, p. 251). According to Cooper and Thakur (2018), regional blocs have become a symbol of a new world order in flux. In Europe, the UK election of December 2019 "produced possibly one of the strongest impacts in European history since World War II and delivered a major blow to the ideal of Europe, to the promotion of a more open and integrated society and the heart of globalization as we have come to know it" (Dieck Assad, 2016, para 1).

The net result of the globalization backlash is a growing skepticism toward the economic theory of global cooperation and the ideological consciousness of the world as a singular entity. Colin Crouch warns of a widespread disillusionment, which could usher in a dangerous era where the world might plunge into "a zero-sum game of regressive economic nationalism" (Crouch, 2019, p. vii). It also signals the departure from the idea of the US-led world order. Developing economies' cultural and political awakening encourages the rise of plural identities (Berggruen & Gardels, 2013). Some predict that "the law of semiglobalization" will reshape the world with more domestic and regional transactions than international ones and that "the law of distance" will strengthen local culture, geography, and economic factors (Ghemawat, 2018, p. 38). International cooperation and global governance are at an "arc of change" (Sell, 2018). New leadership dynamics are taking place that will profoundly impact the structure of the world order and the future of leadership. New forms of influence and power are emerging with the rapid fragmentation and regionalization of the world (Berggruen & Gardels, 2013; Weiss & Wilkinson, 2018).

As the architecture of global governance evolves "towards a visibly pluralistic future, without the traditional dominance of the West" (Cooper & Thakur, 2018, p. 283), there is a new geography of leadership that is emerging with less traditional nongovernmental actors in favor of more connected and disaggregated leadership networks. In this new world order, leadership is expressed through more decentralized and nonhierarchical means, leveraging collective negotiation and vertical engagement with top-down and bottom-up leadership. International organization has favored redistributing global agency to those "governed," creating a new power for followers as a counterpoint to command-and-control leadership approaches.

Global Pandemic

On March 11, 2020, the World Health Organization declared COVID-19 a global pandemic. Two years later (as of August 2022), the coronavirus disease had resulted in 6.5 million confirmed deaths and more than 500 million people infected (WHO, 2022). Experts noted that decades of gains in global health had been erased and that the economic repercussions would be severe and far-reaching across the world for decades (Gavi, 2020). The advent of the disease forced international border closures and led countries to operate in an unprecedented isolationist mode that had not been seen in centuries. In addition to being a health, social, and economic crisis, the impact of the global pandemic on leadership has also been highly significant in shifting leadership perceptions and practices, accelerating networked and virtual leadership approaches, making technology endemic to leading, and changing the nature of leadership goals and outcomes. The future remains uncertain regarding the long-term impact of the coronavirus as a critical test of leadership as well as citizenship, personal freedom, and global cooperation. What is at stake are fundamental choices between nationalist isolation and international solidarity, which will weigh heavily on the future of humankind and leadership as we know it (Harari, 2020).

This shifting global context is creating a new geography of leadership that is critical to acknowledge. In a post-US hegemonic, multipolar, and, more recently, border-controlled world, it is paramount to consider new leadership models that can account for the complexity and variety of methods of influence and management. The idea of "global leadership" has never been further from today's reality. The scene is set for the focus of leadership scholarship to "move beyond the overtly dominant and ethnocentric Western leadership literature and explore Asian leadership based on differing cultural foundations" (Rowley & Ulrich, 2012, p. 451).

References

Alvaredo, F., Atkinson, A. B., Piketty, T., & Saez, E. (2013). The top 1 percent in international and historical perspective. *Journal of Economic Perspectives*, *27*(3), 3–20. https://doi.org/10.1257/jep.27.3.3

Anand, S., Hu, J., Liden, R. C., & Vidyarthi, P. R. (2011). Leader-member exchange: Recent research findings and prospects for the future. In A. Bryman, D. Collinson, K. Grint, G. Jackson, & B. Uhl-Bien (Eds.), *The SAGE handbook of leadership* (pp. 311–325). Sage.

Antonakis, J. (2012). Transformational and charismatic leadership. In D. V. Day & J. Antonakis (Eds.), *The nature of leadership* (2nd ed., pp. 256–288). Sage.

Argyris, C. (1990). *Overcoming organizational defenses: Facilitating organizational learning*. Allyn & Bacon.

Avolio, B. J. (1999). *Full leadership development: Building the vital forces in organizations*. Sage.

Avolio, B. J., Walumbwa, F. O., & Weber, T. J. (2009). Leadership: Current theories, research, and future directions. *Annual Review of Psychology*, *60*(1), 421–449. https://doi.org/10.1146/annurev.psych.60.110707.163621

Barbuto, J. E., & Wheeler, D. W. (2006). Scale development and construct clarification of servant leadership. *Group and Organization Management*, *31*, 300–326. https://doi.org/10.1177/1059601106287090

Bass, B. M. (1985). *Leadership and performance beyond expectation*. Free Press.

Bass, B. M. (1990). *Bass & Stogdill's handbook of leadership: Theory, research and managerial applications*. Free Press.

Bass, B. M. (1998). The ethics of transformational leadership. In J. Ciulla (Ed.), *Ethics: The heart of leadership* (pp. 169–192). Praeger.

Bass, B. M., & Riggio, R. E. (2006). *Transformational leadership* (2nd ed.). Lawrence Erlbaum.

Benioff, M. (2019, October 14). Marc Benioff: We need a new capitalism. *The New York Times*. Retrieved from https://www.nytimes.com/2019/10/14/opinion/benioff-salesforce-capitalism.html

Berggruen, N., & Gardels, N. (2013). *Intelligent governance for the 21st century*. Polity Press.

Bernard, L. L. (1926). *An introduction to social psychology*. Holt and Co.

Bird, A., & Mendenhall, M. E. (2016). From cross-cultural management to global leadership: Evolution and adaptation. *Journal of World Business*, *51*, 115–126.

Bohm, D. (2002). *Wholeness and the implicate order*. Routledge.

Bohm, D. (2004). *On dialogue*. Routledge Great Minds.

Bolden, R., Petrov, G., & Gosling, J. (2008). Tensions in higher education leadership: Towards a multi-level model of leadership practice. *Higher Education Quarterly*, *62*(4), 358–376. https://doi.org/10.1111/j.1468-2273.2008.00398.x

Bowers, D. G., & Seashore, S. E. (1966). Predicting organizational effectiveness with a four-factor theory of leadership. *Administrative Science Quarterly*, *11*, 238–263. https://doi.org/10.2307/2391247

Brown, M. E., Trevino, L., & Harrison, D. A. (2005). Ethical leadership: A social learning perspective for construct development and testing. *Organizational Behavior and Human Performance*, *97*, 117–134. https://doi.org/10.1016/j.obhdp.2005.03.002

Burns, J. M. (1978). *Leadership*. Harper & Row.

Carlyle, T. (1841). *On heroes, hero worship and the heroic in history*. Adams.

Carson, J. B., Tesluk, P. E., & Marrone, J. A. (2007). Shared leadership in teams: An investigation of antecedent conditions and performance. *The Academy of Management Journal*, *50*(5), 1217–1234. https://doi.org/10.2307/20159921

Churchill, W. (1947). The worst form of government. *House of Commons*. Retrieved from https://winstonchurchill.org/resources/quotes/the-worst-form-of-government/

Cooper, A. F., & Thakur, R. (2018). The BRICS in the evolving architecture of global governance. In T. G. Weiss & R. Wilkinson (Eds.), *International Organization and Global Governance* (2nd ed., pp. 283–298). Routledge.

Corbett, F., Fraizer, L., Madjidi, F., & Sweeney, M. (2018). The rise of connectivist leadership. *The IAFOR Research Archive*. http://25qt511nswfi49iayd31ch80-wpengine.netdna-ssl.com/wp-content/uploads/papers/mediasia2018/MediAsia2018_42793.pdf

Cox, R. W. (2018). Critical theory. In T. G. Weiss & R. Wilkinson (Eds.), *International organization and global governance* (2nd ed., pp. 157–169). Routledge.

CQ Researcher (Ed.). (2018). *Global Issues: Selections from CQ Researcher* (1st ed.). CQ Press; an imprint of SAGE Publications.

Crouch, C. (2019). *The globalization backlash*. Polity Press.

Dansereau, F., Graen, G. B., & Haga, W. (1975). A vertical dyad linkage approach to leadership in formal organizations. *Organizational Behavior and Human Performance*, *13*, 46–78. https://doi.org/10.1016/0030-5073(75)90005-7

Day, D. V., Gronn, P., & Salas, E. (2004). Leadership capacity in teams. *Leadership Quarterly*, *15*, 857–880. https://doi.org/10.1016/j.leaqua.2004.09.001

Dent, E. B., Higgins, M. E., & Wharff, D. M. (2005). Spirituality and leadership: An empirical review of definitions, distinctions and embedded assumptions. *The Leadership Quarterly*, *16*, 625–653. https://doi.org/10.1016/j.leaqua.2005.07.002

Dieck Assad, M. (2016, June). Post-Brexit uncertainty, impact, and action. *Global Network for Advanced Management*. https://globalnetwork.io/perspectives/2016/06/post-brexit-uncertainty-impact-and-action

Downton, J. V. (1973). *Rebel leadership: Commitment and charisma in a revolutionary process*. Free Press.

Edelman. (2022). *Edelman trust barometer 2022*. https://www.edelman.com/trust/2022-trust-barometer

Evans, D. (2019). The Holy Bible. In *The Holy Bible*. https://doi.org/10.5040/9781501331732

Evans, M. G. (1970). The effects of supervisory behavior in the path-goal relationship. *Organizational Behavior and Human Performance*, *5*, 277–298. https://doi.org/10.1016/0030-5073(70)90021-8

Evans, M. G. (1996). A path-goal theory of leader effectiveness. *Leadership Quarterly*, *7*(3), 305–309. https://doi.org/10.1016/S1048-9843(96)90021-1

Fernando, M., Beale, F., & Geroy, G. D. (2009). The spiritual dimension in leadership at Dilmah Tea. *Leadership & Organization Development Journal*, *30*(6), 522–539. https://doi.org/10.1108/01437730910981917

Fiedler, F. E. (1964). A contingency model of leadership effectiveness. *Advances in Experimental Social Psychology*, *1*(1964), 149–190. https://doi.org/10.1016/S0065-2601(08)60051-9

Freedom House. (2019). *Freedom in the World 2018: Democracy in crisis*. Retrieved November 24, 2019, from https://freedomhouse.org/report/freedom-world/freedom-world-2018

Fry, L. W. (2003). Toward a theory of spiritual leadership. *The Leadership Quarterly*, *14*, 693–272. https://doi.org/10.1016/j.leaqua.2003.09.001

Fukuyama, F. (1989). *Have we reached the end of history?* Santa Monica. Retrieved from https://www.rand.org/pubs/papers/P7532.htm

Fukuyama, F. (1992). *The end of history and the last man*. Free Press.

Fukuyama, F. (2011a). *Discussion at the Nicolas Berggruen Institute*, Rosewood Sandhill Resort, Menlo Park, CA, December 4, 2011.

Fukuyama, F. (2011b, January 18). US Democracy Has Little to Teach China. *Financial Times*. Retrieved from https://www.ft.com/content/cb6af6e8-2272-11e0-b6a2-00144feab49a

Gavi. (2020, September 30). *Vaccines work*. Gavi.org. https://www.gavi.org/vaccineswork/equality-global-poverty-how-covid-19-affecting-societies-and-economies?gclid=Cj0KCQjw9ZGYBhCEARIsAEUXITWN4rHkhBU6a8IY-6ntBo41WFG-G0y-4E8iQjcHCS0uW2gZhBoUjWAaAp56EALw_wcB

Gerstner, C. R., & Day, D. V. (1997). Meta-Analytic review of leader-member exchange theory: Correlates and construct issues. *Journal of Applied Psychology*, *82*(6), 827–844. https://doi.org/10.1037//0021-9010.82.6.827

Ghemawat, P. (2018). *The new global road map: Enduring strategies for turbulent times*. Harvard Business Review Press.

Gloor, P. A. (2017). *Swarm leadership and the collective mind*. Emerald Publishing.

Goldie, J. G. S. (2016). Connectivism: A knowledge learning theory for the digital age? *Medical Teacher*. https://doi.org/10.3109/0142159X.2016.1173661

Goldsmith, M., Greenberg, C., Robertson, A., & Hu-Chan, M. (2003). *Global leadership: The next generation*. Pearson FT Press.
Graen, G., & Uhl-Bien, M. (1995). Relationship based approach to leadership development of leader-member exchange (LMX) theory of leadership over 25 years: Applying a multi-level multi-domain perspective. *Leadership Quarterly*, 6, 219–247. https://doi.org/10.1016/1048-9843(95)90036-5
Greenleaf, R. K. (1970). *The servant as leader*. The Greenleaf Center for Servant Leadership.
Harari, Y. N. (2020, March 20). Yuval Noah Harari: The world after coronavirus. *Financial Times*. https://www.ft.com/content/19d90308-6858-11ea-a3c9-1fe6fedcca75
Haywood Rolling, J. (2013). *Swarm intelligence: What nature teaches us about shaping creative leadership*. Palgrave Macmillan.
Hazy, J. K., Goldstein, J. A., & Lichtenstein, B. B. (2007). Complex systems leadership theory: An introduction. In J. K. Hazy, J. A. Goldstein, & B. B. Lichtenstein (Eds.), *Complex systems leadership theory: New perspectives from complexity science on social and organizational effectiveness* (pp. 1–13). ISCE Publications.
Hemphill, J., & Coons, A. (1957). Development of the leader behavior description questionnaire. In R. M. Stogdill & A. E. Coons (Eds.), *Leader behavior: Its description and measurement* (pp. 460–463). Columbus Ohio State University, Bureau of Business Research Monograph No. 88.
Hersey, P., & Blanchard, K. H. (1969). Life cycle theory of leadership. *Training & Development*, *23*(5), 26–34.
Herz, M. (2018). Regional governance and regional organizations. In T. G. Weiss & R. Wilkinson (Eds.), *International organization and global governance* (2nd ed., pp. 250–267). Routledge.
House, R. J. (1971). A path-goal theory of leader effectiveness. *Administrative Science Quarterly*, *16*, 321–328. https://doi.org/10.2307/2391905
Jamaludin, Z., Idris, F., Makhbul, Z. K. M., & Rahman, N. M. A. (2011). Do transactional, transformational and spiritual leadership styles distinct? A conceptual insight. *Journal of Global Business and Economics*, 2(1), 73–85. https://doi.org/10.1.1.460.2132&rep=rep1&type=pdf#page=77
Jaworski, J. (2012). *Source: The inner path of knowledge creation*. Berrett-Koehler Publisher.
Jonassen, D., & Land, S. (2012). Preface. In D. Jonassen & S. Land (Eds.), *Theoretical foundations of learning environments* (2nd ed., pp. vii–x). Routledge.
Judge, T. A., & Bono, J. E. (2000). Five-factor model of personality and transformational leadership. *Journal of Applied Psychology*, *85*(5), 751–765. https://doi.org/10.1037/0021-9010.85.5.751
Katz, D., Maccoby, N., & Morse, N. C. (1987). *Productivity, supervision, and morale in an office situation* (part I). Garland. (Original edition 1950).
Katz, R. (1955). Skills of an effective administrator. *Harvard Business Review*, *33*(1), 33–42. https://hbr.org/1974/09/skills-of-an-effective-administrator
Kelly, R. (2019). *Constructing leadership 4.0: Swarm leadership and the fourth industrial revolution*. Palgrave Macmillan. https://doi.org/10.1007/978-3-319-98062-1
Kogler Hill, S. E. (2013). Team leadership. In P. G. Northouse (Ed.), *Leadership: Theory and practice* (6th ed., pp. 287–315). Sage.

Kohs, S. C., & Irle, K. W. (1920). Prophesying army promotion. *Journal of Applied Psychology, 4*(1), 73–87. https://doi.org/10.1037/h0070002

Lambert, L. (2002). *The constructivist leader* (2nd ed.). Teachers College Press.

Lowe, K. B., & Gardner, W. (2001). Ten years of the Leadership Quarterly: Contributions and challenges for the future. *Leadership Quarterly*, *11*(4), 459–514. https://doi.org/10.1016/S1048-9843(00)00059-X

Luthans, F., & Avolio, B. J. (2003). Authentic leadership: A positive developmental approach. In K. Cameron, J. Dutton, & R. Quinn (Eds.), *Positive organizational scholarship: Foundations of a new discipline* (pp. 241–58). Berrett-Koehler.

Mann, R. D. (1959). A review of the relationships between personality and performance in small groups. *Psychological Bulletin.* https://doi.org/10.1037/h0044587

McChesney, C., Covey, S., & Huling, J. (2012). *The 4 disciplines of execution.* Free Press.

Mendenhall, M., Weber, T., Arnardottir, A., & Oddou, G. (2017). Developing global leadership competencies: A process model. *Advances in Global Leadership, 10,* 117–146. https://doi.org/10.1108/S1535-120320170000010004

Northouse, P. G. (2013). *Leadership: Theory and practice* (6th ed.). Sage Publishing.

OECD. (2009). *Growing unequal. Income distribution and poverty in OECD countries.* Organisation for Economic Cooperation and Development.

Palmer, P. (2004). *A hidden wholeness: The journey toward an undivided life.* Jossey-Bass.

Pardo, R. P. (2017). *An analysis of Sun Tzu's the art of war*. Macat Library. https://doi.org/10.4324/9781912282357

Pearce, C., Manz, C. C., & Sims, H. P. (2009). Where do we go from here? Is shared leadership the key to team success? *Organizational Dynamics*, *38*(3), 234–238. https://doi.org/https://doi.org/10.1016/j.orgdyn.2009.04.008

Pearce, C. L., & Conger, J. A. (2003). *Shared leadership: Reframing the hows and whys of leadership*. Sage.

Rajan, R. (2010). *Fault lines: How hidden fractures still threaten the world economy.* University Press.

Rowley, C., & Ulrich, D. (2012). Introduction: Setting the scene for leadership in Asia. *Asia Pacific Business Review*, *18*(4), 451–463. https://doi.org/10.1080/13602381.2012.694726

Safferstone, M. (2005). Organizational leadership: Classic works and contemporary perspectives. *CHOICE: Reviews for Academic Libraries*, 42(6), 959–975. https://doi.org/10.13140/2.1.2412.6084

Sanders, B. (2022, September 2). The US has a ruling class – and Americans must stand up to it. *The Guardian*. https://www.theguardian.com/commentisfree/2022/sep/02/the-us-has-a-ruling-class-and-americans-must-stand-up-to-it

Sell, S. K. (2018). Who governs the globe? In T. G. Weiss & R. Wilkinson (Eds.), *International organization and global governance* (2nd ed., pp. 77–90.). Routledge.

Senge, P. (2006). *The fifth discipline: The art and practice of the learning organization.* Doubleday.

Simonovitz, G., McCoy, J., & Littvay, L. (2021). Democratic hypocrisy and out-group threat: Explaining citizen support for democratic erosion. *The*

Journal of Politics, *84*(3), 1806–1811. https://www.journals.uchicago.edu/doi/10.1086/719009

Sloterdijk, P. (2018). *What happened in the 20th century?* (T. C. Turner, Ed.) (English). Policy Press.

Spears, L. (2002). Tracing the Past, Present, and Future of Servant-Leadership. In L. Spear, & M. Lawrence (Eds.), *Focus on Leadership: Developments in Theory and Research* (pp. 1–16). New York: Palgrave Macmillan.

Strachan, H., & Herberg-Rothe, A. (2008). *Clausewitz in the twenty-first century*. Oxford Scholarship Online. https://doi.org/10.1093/acprof:oso/9780199232024.001.0001

Straus, S., & Driscoll, B. (2019). *International studies: Global forces, interactions, and tensions*. CQ Press; an imprint of SAGE Publications.

Suutari, V. (2002). Global leadership development: An emerging research agenda. *Career Development International*, *7*(4), 218–233.

Trevenna, S., Rappaport, S., Rezmovits, J., & Lowe Steffen, S. (2018). *Evolving leadership for collective well-being: Lessons for implementing the united nations sustainable development goals*. Emerald Publishing Limited.

Uhl-Bien, M., & Marion, R. (2008). *Complexity leadership*. Information Age.

Uhl-Bien, M., Marion, R., & McKelvey, B. (2007). Complexity leadership theory: Shifting leadership from the industrial age to the knowledge era. *The Leadership Quarterly*, *18*, 98–318.

Weiss, T. G., & Wilkinson, R. (2018). *International Organization and Global Governance* (T. G. Weiss & R. Wilkinson, Eds.) (Second). Abingdon: Routledge.

Werfhorst, H. G. Van de, & Salverda, W. (2012). Consequences of economic inequality: Introduction to a special issue? *Social Stratification and Mobility*, *30*, 377–387.

Worthy, B., & Quinn, R. (2017). *An analysis of Niccolò Machiavelli's The Prince*. Macat Library. https://doi.org/10.4324/9781912282241

Yukl, G. (2013). *Leadership in organizations*. Pearson Education Limited.

Zaccaro, S. J., & Bader, P. (2003). E-leadership and the challenges of leading E-teams: Minimizing the bad and maximizing the good. *Organizational Dynamics*, *31*(4), 377–387. https://doi.org/10.1016/S0090-2616(02)00129-8

Zaccaro, S. J., Heinen, B., & Shuffler, M. (2009). Team leadership and team effectiveness. In E. Salas, G. F. Goodwin, & C. S. Burke (Eds.), *Team effectiveness in complex organizations: Cross-disciplinary perspectives and approaches* (pp. 83–111). Taylor and Francis Group.

Zhu, W., Avoloio, B. J., Riggio, R. E., & Sosik, J. J. (2011). The effect of authentic transformational leadership on follower and group ethics. *Leadership Quarterly*, *22*, 801–817. https://doi.org/10.1016/j.leaqua.2011.07.004

Zigurs, I. (2003). Leadership in virtual teams: Oxymoron or opportunity? *Organizational Dynamics*, *31*(4), 339–351. https://doi.org/10.1016/S0090-2616(02)00132-8

2 The Rise of Asia

New Economic Powerhouse

The cartography of leadership has been redrawn with the rise of Asia, which is establishing itself as a new economic powerhouse. According to Mc. Kinsey & Company (2015), the world economy is going through a major disruption resulting from the confluence of four fundamental and disruptive forces: (1) a shift of the world's economic activity to the East, (2) the acceleration of technological change, (3) an aging population, and (4) Asia becoming the world's largest trading region with flows of capital, people, data, and communication. Woetzel and Jeogmin (2019) contend that the global center of gravity is shifting toward Asia and that it is paramount to now operate in an "Asianized world."

After the end of the Cold War, the United States used its growing economic power to exert influence on international organization and to shape global governance through the establishment of institutions, rules, and ideologies that favored its self-interests (Knight, 2018). In the last decade, however, the United States faced increased pressure economically from the rise of regional governance actors such as the European Union (EU) and the BRICS (Brazil, Russia, India, China, and South Africa). Notably, Asia is rapidly establishing itself as a new economic powerhouse on the world stage, with several countries experiencing significant economic growth in recent years. Among the countries that are leading the charge in this regard are China, India, and Indonesia, which are all known for their large populations and solid economic indicators alongside the small but mighty island state of Singapore.

According to the latest revision by the United Nations, the world population reached 8 billion people on November 15, 2022, with Asia accounting for about half of all people around the globe (United Nations, 2019). China has the largest population of any country in the world, with more than 1.4 billion people (CIA World Factbook, 2020b). India is not far behind, with a population of over 1.3 billion people (CIA World Factbook,

DOI: 10.4324/9781003399377-5

2020a). Indonesia has the fourth largest population in the world, with over 270 million people (CIA World Factbook, 2020a, 2020b). These large populations are a crucial factor in the rise of Asia as they provide a vast pool of potential workers and consumers. This growth allows for economies of scale, which drives down the cost of production and makes goods and services more affordable for consumers.

Strong economic indicators reflect the significant growth that these Asian countries have experienced in recent years. China has established itself as a superpower in the last ten years, competing directly with the United States. Since the 1978 reforms by Deng Xiaoping and the dramatic acceleration of the 1990s, China has been touted as an "economic miracle" (Ray, 2002). In China, the economy has been growing at an average rate of more than 6% per year for the past three decades, with robust growth in sectors such as manufacturing and services (World Bank, 2021). Presently, China has the second largest economy in the world, with a Gross Domestic Product (GDP) of more than $13 trillion in 2019 (World Bank, 2021). In India, the economy has also been growing at a robust pace, averaging around 7% per year over the past decade (World Bank, 2021). India has the fifth largest economy, with a GDP of about $2.9 trillion in 2019 (World Bank, 2021). Indonesia has the 16th largest economy, with a GDP of around $1.1 trillion in 2019 (World Bank, 2021), while Singapore has the 33rd largest economy, with a GDP of approximately $350 billion in 2019 (World Bank, 2021). Singapore has a disproportionately strong economy given its small population (5.7 million people, according to the CIA World Factbook, 2020a, 2020b) compared to other Asian countries. This is due to several factors, including the country's highly developed and advanced economy, its strategic location at the crossroads of Asia, and its strong institutions and policies.

One of the key drivers of economic growth in China and India has been the rapid development of their domestic consumer markets. As incomes have risen and living standards have improved, more and more people in these countries can afford consumer goods and services that were previously out of reach. Demand for products such as smartphones, cars, and appliances has surged, fueling growth in the manufacturing and services sectors.

In addition to their large populations and strong economic indicators, another critical factor in the rise of Asia as an economic powerhouse is the innovation and technology being developed in these countries. Asia has fostered the proliferation of technology-enabled business models, from online retail platforms like Alibaba to car-hailing apps like Grab, which bought Uber in parts of Southeast Asia. Digital technology, networked cities, offices, and people promise economic progress and profound leadership transformation in emerging economies that have leapfrogged directly to always-on connectivity from their mobile phones, with new ways to live, work, and play. As a result, Asia is home to 50% of the world's fastest growing companies, which have increased their capitalizations by more than ten times over the past decade (Ihara & Cho, 2019). China, for example, has become a world leader in fields such as robotics and renewable energy and is investing heavily in these areas to maintain its competitive edge (Chui, 2022).

Moreover, China has risen to the number two position in artificial intelligence (AI) and announced its ambition to be the world leader by 2030, backed by aggressive government funding and research centers in Beijing and Tianjin (Fabian, 2018). In 2019, China gained more companies on the Fortune Global 500 list than the United States, which saw its number of companies decline from 126 to 121 (Yangpeng, 2019). Meanwhile, India is known for its software development and biotechnology strengths and is investing heavily in life sciences to become an innovation hub (FICCI, 2020). Indonesia and Singapore are also known for their investments in innovation and technology. Indonesia, for example, has a rapidly growing tech sector, with many start-ups and established companies focusing on areas such as e-commerce, Fintech, and digital health (McKinsey & Company, 2016). Singapore's highly developed and advanced economy, with a well-educated and skilled workforce, has fueled advances in biotech, clean tech, and smart cities (EDB Singapore, 2018). Singapore has also invested heavily in research and development and has a thriving innovation ecosystem. These factors have enabled the country to compete on the world stage despite its relatively small population.

Another critical factor in the rise of Asia is the growing integration of the region's economies. China, in particular, has been actively promoting regional economic integration through initiatives such as the Belt and Road Initiative, which aims to connect Asia, Europe, and Africa through a network of infrastructure projects. This approach has helped to boost trade and investment within the region. One of the key beneficiaries of this growing economic integration has been Indonesia, which is strategically located at the crossroads of Asia and well positioned to take advantage of the increased trade and investment flows resulting from the Belt and Road Initiative. Indonesia also benefits from the growing middle class in countries like China and India, providing new markets for Indonesian exports.

Finally, these countries foster new economic power by investing heavily in research and development (R&D). In China, for example, the government has set a target of reaching 2.5% of GDP in R&D spending by 2020, up from 1.4% in 2015 (National Bureau of Statistics of China, 2015). In India, the government has also increased its R&D spending in recent years, intending to reach 2% of the GDP by 2020 (Department of Science and Technology, 2019).

Leadership Experimentation

The rise of Asia as a new economic powerhouse on the world stage has created opportunities for alternative leadership approaches and experimentation. As these countries have become more economically powerful, they have begun to develop new business models and management methods that best serve their interests and priorities rather than merely copying Western approaches.

One of the ways this has manifested itself is in the economic policies of Asian countries. Many countries in the region, including China, India, and Indonesia, have embraced state-led economic development strategies, prioritizing domestic growth and development over global integration and free trade. This protectionist approach to trade and investment has meant that these countries seek to nurture their industries and build up their domestic markets. This independence is also evident in the foreign policy approaches of Asian countries. For example, China has become increasingly assertive in pursuing its interests on the world stage, particularly in the South China Sea. This offensive stance and other territorial disputes with its neighbors are creating tensions with the United States and other Western powers, which have traditionally been the dominant powers in the region. Meanwhile, India has also sought to assert itself globally and adopted a more independent foreign policy approach in recent years. India has traditionally been a close ally of the United States but increasingly sought to build ties with other countries, such as Russia and China, to balance its relations with the major traditional power players.

As Asian countries have become more economically powerful, they have also asserted their own leadership approaches and locally relevant systems. The growth of privately owned companies in the region has created a step change in leadership versus state-owned enterprises (SOEs). Many countries in the area, including China, India, and Indonesia, have prominent and influential SOEs that play a significant role in their economies. These SOEs often have close ties to the government and are used as a tool to promote economic growth and development. Leadership approaches between SOEs and privately owned companies are markedly different in Asia. SOEs are typically more hierarchical and bureaucratic in their management structures and are often subject to political influence and interference.

In contrast, privately owned companies in Asia are now focusing on innovation and entrepreneurship. They are adopting more flexible and agile management styles to compete in a rapidly changing business environment. As the region has become more economically powerful, there has been a growing emphasis on creating value for customers and shareholders and challenging traditional business and leadership models. One example of this is the rise of the tech sector in Asia. Countries like China, India, and Indonesia have seen the emergence of many start-ups and established companies focused on areas such as e-commerce, Fintech, and digital health. These companies are often led by young, dynamic leaders willing to take risks and work in agile ways.

Another key growth area in Asia from privately owned companies is a focus on sustainability and social responsibility. As incomes have risen and living standards have improved in the region, there has been a growing awareness of the need to address issues such as climate change, inequality, and poverty. Many companies in Asia are now incorporating sustainability and social responsibility into their business models and are working to create value for society by focusing on purposeful leadership.

Furthermore, innovative companies in Asia have learned to rely on technology and networked leadership approaches to drive growth and competitiveness. Innovation often requires a willingness to embrace change and challenge the status quo. Technology and networked leadership approaches are well suited to facilitating this dynamic and adaptive thinking. Many of the countries in the region are undergoing rapid economic and social transformation and are facing complex and dynamic challenges that require innovative and adaptable solutions. Asian business leaders are responding to these challenges by adopting more collaborative and team-based leadership styles.

In many cases, leaders in Asia are more willing to delegate authority and empower their teams and are more open to input and ideas from others. Many countries in the region are at the forefront of the digital revolution. They are developing and adopting new technologies at a rapid pace. More connected and networked organizations have enabled leaders in Asia to leverage technology to facilitate real-time collaboration and communication within their teams and support e-leadership approaches through digital tools and platforms. Companies are also using data and analytics to manage workflows more seamlessly and efficiently with virtual coordination and distributed decision-making, enabling teams to respond more quickly and effectively to changing market conditions.

The more innovative companies in Asia are characterized by a high degree of decentralization and empowerment, with leaders encouraging and enabling their teams to take ownership of their work and contribute their ideas and insights. Networked leadership facilitates collaboration and communication within teams and organizations. In a networked leadership model, leaders are less commanding and controlling their teams and instead more focused on facilitating collaboration and idea sharing among team members. In contrast to more traditional leadership approaches, there is an emphasis on technology and digital tools to encourage teams to leverage the collective intelligence and expertise of the entire organization.

This approach is well suited to Asia's fast-paced and dynamic business environment and is helping to drive innovation and growth in the region.

Leadership Divergence

The rise of Asia accelerates and accentuates a global movement of divergence politically, economically, and in leadership. According to Martin Wolf (2011), economies that used to be at the periphery are re-emerging as the core force transforming the world economy. He explains that former colonies are on a rapid growth path toward economic advantage, reversing the nineteenth- and early twentieth-century trend of western European dominance (Wolf, 2011). In 2000, Kenneth Pomeranz wrote about *The Great Divergence,* describing the growing inequalities between the Western world and the East during the late eighteenth and nineteenth centuries (Pomeranz, 2000). In the 1980s, the term was replaced by the great "convergence," as most emerging countries reached economic growth rates significantly higher than most developed countries (Korotayev et al., 2015). Nobel economist Michael Spence further reinforced this point observing that the significant discrepancies between advanced and developing countries are rapidly declining for the first time in 250 years. Notably, there is a pattern of convergence, where the future of economic growth is found in a multispeed world favoring developing countries and those previously known as the "governed" (Spence, 2011).

Today's world order is no longer based on "a concentration of power" (Clark, 2011) or on hegemony, which conceptualizes the world order by institutionalizing inequality and privilege. No one power now exerts total coercive ability, control, and dominance. With the end of colonialization and the fading of Western influence, the world order has shifted. Bipolar geopolitics based on superiority and subordination are being retired with a new form of *Sustainable Leadership* based on "multilevel systems thinking, which integrates economic, societal, and environmental factors" and multilateral stakeholder inclusion (Murphy, 2022, p. 8). Hegemons enforcing their rules, norms, and ideas are increasingly questioned and challenged. The current international system favors the redistribution of global agency with an interdependence of plural identities, cultural divergence, and leadership based on followership and legitimacy rather than coercion. "We may be moving towards a post-hegemonic world in which there will be no single overarching dominant power" (Knight, 2018, p. 320), neither from the US nor a Chinese hegemon.

The new geography of leadership and the redistribution of global agency culminate in a new era described by many as "multipolar." Henry Kissinger predicted that the twenty-first century's international system would comprise at least six major powers (US, China, India, Japan, Russia, and EU) and a collection of various sized countries participating in global governance (Kissinger, 1994). In this redrawn cartography of leadership, Samuel Huntington has stressed the importance of cultural identities as the single most crucial factor in the balance of power globally, which has become "multicivilizational" (Huntington, 2011). He argues that an emerging "civilization-based world order" will become more important than ideologies, political, and economic zones and provide groupings of leadership based on cultural kinship (Huntington, 2011). This idea can spur new forms of leadership with rich and developing countries cooperating based on cultural affinity and participating in global governance equally using different and diverse models.

References

Chui, D. (2022). *The east is green: China's global leadership in renewable energy*. Center for Strategic & International Studies. https://www.csis.org/east-green-chinas-global-leadership-renewable-energy

CIA World Factbook. (2020a). *China*. https://www.cia.gov/library/publications/the-world-factbook/geos/ch.html

CIA World Factbook. (2020b). *India*. https://www.cia.gov/library/publications/the-world-factbook/geos/in.html

Clark, I. (2011). China and the United States: A succession of hegemonies? *International Affairs*, 87(1), 1424.

Department of Science and Technology. (2019). *India's R&D expenditure & scientific publications on the rise*. https://dst.gov.in/indias-rd-expenditure-scientific-publications-rise

EDB Singapore. (2018). *Singapore's economic development board: Overview*. https://www.edb.gov.sg/

Fabian. (2018). *Global artificial intelligence landscape | including database with 3,465 AI companies*. Retrieved November 3, 2019, from https://medium.com/@bootstrappingme/global-artificial-intelligence-landscape-including-database-with-3-465-ai-companies-3bf01a175c5d

FICCI. (2020). *Reshaping India into a life sciences innovation hub*. https://ficci.in/spdocument/23185/Reshaping-India-into-a-life-sciences-innovation-hub.pdf

Huntington, S. P. (2011). *The clash of civilizations and the remaking of world order*. Simon & Schuster Paperbacks.

Ihara, K., & Cho, Y. (2019, May 9). Asia is home to 50% of the world's fastest growing companies. *Nikkei Asian Review*. https://asia.nikkei.com/Business/Companies/Asia-is-home-to-50-of-world-s-fastest-growing-companies2

Kissinger, H. (1994). *Diplomacy*. Simon & Schuster.

Knight, A. (2018). US hegemony. In T. G. Weiss & R. Wilkinson (Eds.), *International organization and global governance* (2nd ed., pp. 311–324). Routledge.

Korotayev, A., Zinkina, J., & Goldstone, J. (2015). Phases of global demographic transition correlate with phases of the great divergence and great convergence. *Technological Forecasting & Social Change*, 95, 163–169. Retrieved from https://

www.academia.edu/12812235/Phases_of_global_demographic_transition_correlate_with_phases_of_the_Great_Divergence_and_Great_Convergence

Mc. Kinsey & Company. (2015). The four global forces breaking all the trends. In R. Dobbs, J. Manyika, & J. Woetzel (Eds.), *No Ordinary Disruption: The Four Global Forces Breaking All the Trends*. PublicAffairs. https://www.andrewleunginternationalconsultants.com/files/the_four_global_forces_breaking_all_the_trends.pdf

McKinsey & Company. (2016). *Unlocking Indonesia's digital opportunity.* https://www.mckinsey.com/~/media/McKinsey/Locations/Asia/Indonesia/Our%20Insights/Unlocking%20Indonesias%20digital%20opportunity/Unlocking_Indonesias_digital_opportunity.ashx#:~:text=By%20going%20digital%2C%20Indonesia%20can, benefits%20in%20the%20long%20run

Murphy, C. (2022). *Sustainable leadership, lessons of vision, courage, and grit from the CEOs who dared to build a better world* (1st ed.). Wiley.

National Bureau of Statistics of China. (2015). *China Statistical Yearbook 2015.* http://www.stats.gov.cn/tjsj/ndsj/2015/indexeh.htm

Pomeranz, K. (2000). *The great divergence: China, Europe, and the making of the modern world economy (The Princeton economic history of the Western world).* Princeton University Press.

Ray, A. (2002). The Chinese economic miracle: Lessons to be learnt. *Economic and Political Weekly*, *37*(37), 3835–3848. http://www.jstor.org/stable/4412606

Spence, M. (2011). *The next convergence: The future of economic growth in a multispeed world* (1st ed.). Farrar, Straus and Giroux.

United Nations. (2019). *World population prospects 2019.* United Nations DESA/Population. https://population.un.org

Woetzel, J., & Jeogmin, S. (2019, October). The Asianized world has arrived. *Project Syndicate.* https://www.project-syndicate.org/commentary/asian-century-economic-rise-regional-integration-by-jonathan-woetzel-and-jeongmin-seong-2019-10

Wolf, M. (2011). In the grip of a great convergence. *Financial Times.* Retrieved from https://www.ft.com/content/072c87e6-1841-11e0-88c9-00144feab49a

World Bank. (2021). *Data: GDP (current US$).* https://data.worldbank.org/indicator/NY.GDP.MKTP.CD

Yangpeng, Z. (2019). In a first, China has more companies on *Fortune* global 500 list than the US. *South China Morning Post.* https://www.scmp.com/business/companies/article/3019632/first-china-has-more-companies-fortune-global-500-list-us

3 The Network Imperative

Decentralization

In recent decades, dramatic technological advances, particularly associated with high-speed information and data networks, have restructured time and space and the boundaries of ideas, production, and human exchange (Kirsch, 1995). The popular concept of a "shrinking world" is a by-product of telecommunications, information, and transportation innovations. Notably, technology's role in transforming time–space compression is not limited to the physical aspect. It has also altered how social relations and leadership are spatialized at a new scale of experience. With the rapid advances in technology and communications, leaders can condense time and location, operating at a new meta-level that allows them to be connected, disaggregated, and virtual. Leaders become "boundary spanners, bridge makers, and blenders of culture" (Zander et al., 2012, p. 592), needing to leverage greater diversity than ever.

Politically, Addis (2004) postulates that the communication revolution has eroded the concept of national sovereignty and that we are witnessing the rise of "the thin state" against the backdrop of a decentralized system of governance and transborder information flows. With the rapid advances in technology and communications, leaders of nations and the private sector can compress time and location, operating at a new meta-level that allows them to be connected and disaggregated. Sell (2018) notes the growing importance of transnational networks displacing traditional state-centric modes of governance, allowing for indirect methods of influence and advocacy, both challenging and correcting institutional authority. The operation of networks beyond national lines and at all levels of power – presidents, diplomats, prosecutors, law enforcement, and local citizens – has created new "power circuits" (Edwards, 2016) with amorphous leadership systems and flows of illicit activity in the form of transnational organized crime (TOC) and terrorist organizations.

DOI: 10.4324/9781003399377-6

Transparency

Social networks and the pervasive use of always-on technology have been "a game-changer" for governance in the twenty-first century (Berggruen & Gardels, 2013). Mobile phones connected to the internet have given every person on the planet participatory power and the ability to challenge governing authorities asking for more transparency and real-time responsiveness. The "Arab Spring" revolutionary movement in the Middle East and North Africa between 2010 and 2012 has spurred the rise of social networks and people's ability to organize demonstrations and protests through spontaneous undetectable information networks. Decades back, Alvin Toffler remarked that knowledge was the primary source of wealth in our time (Toffler, 1987). Most assumptions about leadership in a new global governance environment are outdated: "We're in a knowledge economy, but our managerial and governance systems are stuck in the Industrial Era" (Uhl-Bien et al., 2007, p. 298).

Realism has traditionally been a dominant school of thought in international relations theory, with the understanding that leadership occurs through power distribution based on the role of states and national interest in world politics. Today, network theory is becoming increasingly relevant with the diffusion of political authority and global governance (Madsen, 2018). The use of networks indicates a new distribution of global leadership with a plurality of relations, self-organized influence systems, and resilient, agile relationships. Decentralized power and leaderless systems (Brafman & Beckstrom, 2006) provide a new framework for understanding leadership. According to Johansen (2017), the next decade will be a pivotal moment in time as digital connectivity amplifies and everything becomes "distributed" (p. ix). Every person will be connected and have pervasive internet access to experience a blended reality that is part physical and part virtual.

Organic Organizational Systems

In *The Network Imperative*, authors Barry Libert, Megan Beck, and Jerry Wind (2016) argue that digital networks are also changing business rules. Amazon, Google, and Uber are not just companies; they are digital platforms providing scalable, data-led networked business models that create value by building networks of employees, customers, and suppliers worldwide. In these conditions, expecting the same leadership theories and practices is misguided.

During most of the early nineteenth century, traditional hierarchical organizational models dominated (see Figure 3.1) with the characteristics

The Mechanistic System

- Specialized differentiation of functional tasks
- A hierarchical structure of control, authority, and communication
- A tendency for interaction between members to be vertical (i.e., between superior and subordinate)
- A tendency for operations and working behavior to be governed by instructions and decisions issued by superiors
- Negotiation of tasks done by immediate superiors
- Authority dictated by hierarchical position

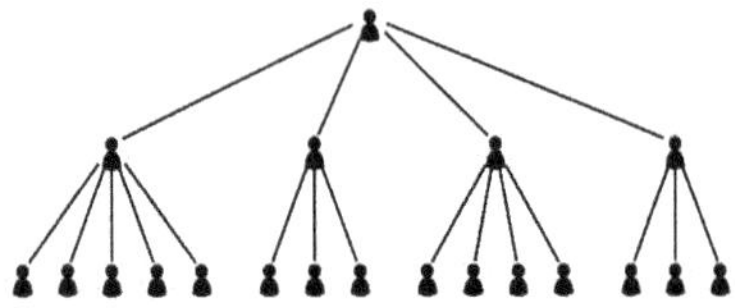

Figure 3.1 Characteristics of the Mechanistic Organizational System.

Source: Reprinted from Anderson, D. (2019). *Organization Design: Creating Strategic & Agile Organizations*. Thousand Oaks, CA: Sage. Copyright 2019 by Sage Publications Inc. Picture from Lumen. (2020). Organizational Behavior / Human Relations: Organic versus Mechanistic Models. Retrieved May 3, 2020, from https://courses.lumenlearning.com/wm-organizationalbehavior/chapter/organic-versus-mechanistic-models/. Reprinted with permission.

of mechanistic systems (Burns & Stalker, 1961). Centralized factory-based, scientific, and bureaucratic organizations promoted organizational structures that were predictable, highly engineered, and based on power and order (Burns & Stalker, 1961). Tasks were highly specialized, and the interactions between leaders and subordinates were vertically delineated. Companies were managed like integrated machines with predetermined structures, governance, processes, and highly regulated norms across workers and superiors.

In mechanistic systems, leadership was dictated by institutionalized authority based on hierarchical position with the use of dominance and coercion, exclusively at the direction of the heroic leader to fit the organization's needs. "Historically, leadership has been conceived around a single individual – the leader – and how that person inspires, entices, commands, cajoles, and controls followers. This idea has been the dominant paradigm of leadership for many, many decades" (Pearce et al., 2009, p. 234).

Post-World War II, the world emerged from mass production with closed, hierarchical, and rational organizational models. With rapid global growth, leaders embraced more flexible structures that manifested the characteristics of organic systems in contrast to mechanistic systems (Burns & Stalker, 1961). As a result, organizations migrated from predictable engineering structures to approaches that allowed them to respond more quickly to rapidly changing technological, economic, and competitive environments. Instead of specialized and delineated tasks, individual jobs became more loosely defined with more informal structures. Allen et al. (1998) noted that "the old organizational pyramids of the nineteenth century are crumbling, being replaced by upside-down pyramids and circles and connections" (p. 575; see Figure 3.2).

The Organic System

• Individual job broadly defined, not self-contained
• A network structure of control, authority, and communication
• A lateral rather than vertical direction of communication through the organization, communication between people of different rank, resembling consultation rather than command
• Content of communication consists of information and advice rather than instructions and decisions
• Adjustment and continual redefinition of individual tasks through interaction with others
• Authority decided by whomever is most informed and capable

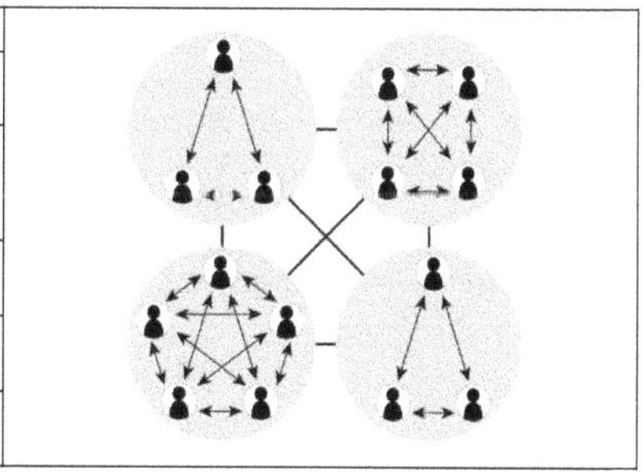

Figure 3.2 Characteristics of the Organic Organizational System.

Source: Reprinted from Anderson, D. (2019). *Organization Design: Creating Strategic & Agile Organizations.* Thousand Oaks, CA: Sage. Copyright 2019 by Sage Publications Inc. Picture from Lumen. (2020). Organizational Behavior / Human Relations: Organic versus Mechanistic Models. Retrieved May 3, 2020, from https://courses.lumenlearning.com/wm-organizationalbehavior/chapter/organic-versus-mechanistic-models/. Reprinted with permission.

The implications of organic organizational systems are far-reaching for promoting emerging post-heroic leadership approaches. With organic systems, leadership shifts from a direct command to consultation and collaboration. A network structure of communication replaces the hierarchical structure of control and authority from the mechanistic system. The interaction between members of the organization moves from vertical to lateral as communication occurs in all directions. As a result, all levels are enabled and a more consultative, collaborative stream of information becomes possible. An important outcome of this societal transformation is the desire for everyone to be a leader, with followers recast as equal contributors (Maccoby, 2007).

Networked Learning

In addition to changing the structure and nature of organizations, the digital world has metamorphosed learning. Where knowledge resides, and how it is transmitted, is now data-led. Information is no longer the privilege of the few as knowledge circulates across open platforms open to all. At the same time, through digital networks, anyone can share their insights and experience globally, collaborating with others in the digital space. The evolution of learning theories provides an excellent insight into our changing understanding of knowledge and the impact of the network imperative on learning.

Traditional learning theories captured conventional thinking on learning as externally motivated and determined. They viewed knowledge as absolute and unchanging and a process of pure memorization. Knowledge was centralized in the teacher, while students were passive recipients in a relationship defined by authority and obedience. Learning was not democratic but based on the teacher–student power dynamic, hierarchy, and fostering compliance to set standards. In contrast, the learning theory of connectivism, introduced in 2004, challenged traditional learning theories – behaviorism, cognitivism, humanism, and constructivism – and addressed how learning occurred differently in the digital age (Siemens, 2005a). Siemens (2005a) denounced the boundaries of previous learning theories noting that they were developed before the advent of social networking technologies, which rendered many of their ideas obsolete. Downes (2007) also added to the thinking on Connectivism. He declared that "at its heart, connectivism is the thesis that knowledge is distributed across a network of connections, and therefore that learning consists of the ability to construct and traverse those networks" (para. 1).

As one of the most recent and modern learning theories, Connectivism is the only approach recognizing learning as a process of creating networks and the human activity within these networks (Siemens, 2005a). In this modern construct, learning is informal and can occur through the many ways individuals naturally socialize in communities of practice and personal networks. Focusing on networks, Connectivism establishes that the learner belongs to a community, which enriches the group with intelligence and new data (Siemens, 2005a, 2005b). Growing connections and nodes enable continuous dialogue and meaning-making. Siemens argued that the learning theory of Connectivism had far-reaching implications for "all aspects of life" beyond instructional environments, including organizations and especially leadership, which needed to be reexamined within a network ecology (Siemens, 2005a).

In summary, the world is reckoning with a new network imperative. The digital age decentralizes information, provides radical transparency, encourages data-led networked business models, and facilitates networked learning. Surviving and growing in this context requires adapting to network-based ways of thinking, behaving and leading.

References

Addis, A. (2004). The thin state in thick globalism: Sovereignty in the information age. *Vanderbilt Journal of Transnational Law*, *37*(1), 1–107.

Allen, K., Bordas, J., Robinson Hickman, G., Matusak, L. R., Sorenson, G. J., & Whitemire, K. J. (1998). Leadership in the 21st century. In G. Robinson Hickman (Ed.), *Leading organizations: Perspectives for a new era* (pp. 572–580). Sage Publications.

Anderson, D. (2019). *Organization design: Creating strategic and agile organizations*. Sage.

Berggruen, N., & Gardels, N. (2013). *Intelligent governance for the 21st century*. Polity Press.

Brafman, O., & Beckstrom, R. A. (2006). *The starfish and the spider: The unstoppable power of leadersless organizations*. Portfolio.

Burns, T., & Stalker, G. M. (1961). *The management of innovation*. Tavistock.

Downes, S. (2007, February). *What connectivism is*. [Blog]. https://www.downes.ca/post/38653

Edwards, A. (2016). Multi-centered governance and circuits of power in liberal modes of security. *Global Crime*, *17*(3–4), 240–263.

Johansen, R. (2017). *The new leadership literacies: Thriving in a future of extreme disruption and distributed everything* (1st ed.). Berrett-Koehler.

Kirsch, S. (1995). The incredible shrinking world? Technology and the production of space. *Environment and Planning D: Society & Space*, *13*, 529–555. http://citeseerx.ist.psu.edu /viewdoc/download?doi=10.1.1.455.1446&rep=rep1&type=pdf

Libert, B., Beck, M., & Wind, J. (2016). *The network imperative*. Harvard Business Review Press.

Maccoby, M. (2007). *The leaders we need and what makes us follow*. Harvard Business School Press.

Madsen, F. G. (2018). Transnational criminal networks. In T. G. Weiss & R. Wilkinson (Eds.), *International organization and global governance* (2nd ed., pp. 437–449). Routledge.

Sell, S. K. (2018). Who governs the globe? In T. G. Weiss & R. Wilkinson (Eds.), *International organization and global governance* (2nd ed., pp. 77–90.). Routledge.

Siemens, G. (2005a). Connectivism: A learning theory for the digital age. *International Journal of Instructional Technology & Distance Learning*, 2005, 1–9. https://jotamac.typepad.com/jotamacs_weblog/files/Connectivism.pdf

Siemens, G. (2005b, August 10). *Connectivism: Learning as network-creation*. Elearnspace.org. http://masters.donntu.org/2010/fknt/lozovoi/library/article4.htm

Toffler, A. (1987). *The third wave*. Random House.

Uhl-Bien, M., Marion, R., & McKelvey, B. (2007). Complexity leadership theory: Shifting leadership from the industrial age to the knowledge era. *The Leadership Quarterly*, *18*, 98–318.

Zander, L., Mockaitis, A. I., & Butler, C. L. (2012). Leading global teams. *Journal of World Business, 47*(4), 592–603. https://doi.org/10.1016/j.jwb.2012.01.012

Part I
Conclusion

Conclusion

A new geography of leadership is unfolding. The world is shifting away from a unified globalist ideology and a dominant Western view of leadership informed by a single discourse. Fundamental geopolitical dynamics are at play in changing the world: anti-globalization, democratic erosion, distrust in capitalism, regionalization, localization, and pressure resulting from the global pandemic. The emergence of Asia as a new global power player in a more multipolar world is affording a divergence of concepts on leadership, where newer economies that used to be at the periphery are emerging as new voices to contend with for the future. Networking technologies are transforming the leadership of nations through a surge of decentralization and transparency; the structure of organizations is moving to organic networked systems; and knowledge is now recognized as a network-forming process, resulting in new ways of connected learning and teaching.

Research findings presented in the upcoming Part 2 should be understood against this dramatically changing global landscape.

DOI: 10.4324/9781003399377-7

Part II

Asia – Future Leadership Sandbox

- "Many large conglomerate families want to innovate and want to change. Right. They know the importance of investing in digital transformation, but yeah, the old guard says, 'We're still making money, so fine.'" (Participant #18)
- "Older organizations are more hierarchical and less collaborative, more directive. It's definitely less about the emotional connectedness to individuals. It's never binary, but I think on a spectrum, it's a little bit more task versus emotion." (Participant #8)

Networking Technology

The impact of technology on leadership in Asia was described as foundational, just like that of culture. Technology was seen as a key pillar of business activity and an essential tool:

- "Google today is a public utility; Facebook today is a public utility. It's no different than the power utility. The reality is when 100% of a society derives meaningful utility from your use; you are a public utility." (Participant #3)
- "We all need to understand with social media, with the internet and all this technology, everything, whether your industry is in tech or not, is going to go digital. It's a fundamental shift. And so, what that means is that our worldview really has to incorporate this absolute change." (Participant #15)
- "I feel that technology in the past was used more as a luxury. But now, we need technology for us to still continue to work together and for us to connect. So, if we didn't have the technology, I would imagine we would have a massive economic collapse." (Expert #1)

Technology's impact on leadership was profound; it extended further than being the main gateway to information and creating efficiency gains. Technology was described as a paradigm-shifting force that leaders were leveraging to build new digitally enabled business models:

- "In Asia, there's a lot of the leading by scale. Jack Ma, as leader, has made a huge influence in China with the economy and e-commerce. The whole technology infrastructure has that scale to connect the dots and influence a whole new generation. I think it's quite a phenomenon." (Participant #11)
- "Now game-changing ideas can be achieved using technology." (Participant #5)
- "It's become easy for people to shift from one thing to the other, to be able to give up their jobs, their zip code, and to be able to dream of

starting things on their own right and become an entrepreneur." (Participant #9)
- "Technology has really accelerated our options for farmer engagement. In places in China, where the broadband is relatively good, even in the rural areas, we're able to do farmer engagement by video. We basically retrain females and do demonstrations in the field with a selfie video. And it's been amazing to see thousands of farmers logging in to watch that. In fact, now the discussion is how much of what we've learned in this big experiment should we take forward in the future for new business ideas." (Participant #22)

Technology was enabling a new level playing field by empowering everyone, everywhere:

- "I feel like, in a way, it helps level up the playing field. As I mentioned earlier, right, I guess a lot of the knowledge is actually with people that are younger, less experienced, so it makes it easier to share their opinions." (Participant #28)
- "I think technology empowers everyone; it gives them the means to live their lives in a way that will make them happiest and at the same time to deliver the objectives that they've signed up for." (Participant #1)
- "I don't see any differences between Millennials in Indonesia and in the United States because, with the internet, they share common values in terms of their ability to use technology, to be creative, because every night, everyone now can be a singer on YouTube, everyone now can be a writer, everyone can be an influencer, a photographer for Instagram. I think the level playing field is the same." (Participant #12)
- "The internet is the first medium that we've ever participated in as a society that's a two-way medium. And by its very nature, the fact that the internet is participatory has shifted power from the producers to the consumers in a way that's undeniable. People realize they have agency and empowerment." (Participant #3)
- "Technology is changing how we interact and is making things more content driven. There's more substance; ideas become more important than seniority or rank because how we interact is more faceless. The content and ideas have more power than the person who said them. We're all empowered." (Participant #29)

Furthermore, technology was deepening the relationships of people and the quality of their connections by connecting physical, social, and emotional dimensions:

- "So obviously we use technology now to stay in touch. Right. You know, I've always been a really huge believer that technology can

enable connection. As long as it enables deeper connections." (Participant #5)
- "To really connect to everything, to people, to commerce, to payments." (Participant #11)
- "There is no power distance, which means that everyone can reach you and everyone can ask you questions. Everyone can say something to you at any time." (Participant #12)
- "It helps make us more connected. It helps the transfer of knowledge but also the transfer of emotion." (Participant #24)
- "With technology, there's been an even greater need for human contact, a greater need for insight, for just the humanity that we can add at a very visceral primal level and that we crave. So, what leaders are having to do is negotiate the twin channel of running their business in a highly efficient way using technology to make decisions or get stuff done, and at the same time paying attention to people, their hearts and minds." (Expert #6)

For all its merits, technology was also decried for certain negative aspects, all of which were primarily related to how it could damage human relationships: concentrating power and influence, creating weak ties, inhibiting creativity, reducing spontaneity, and creating distractions and exhaustion. Overall, the influence of technology on leadership was significant and instrumental in creating a new leadership phenomenon. With more democratized information, empowerment, and deeper connections, technology was supporting more distributed, collective, and digitally enabled forms of leadership:

- "Leaders are standing at an intersection for leadership, working with big data, cloud computing, and artificial intelligence. I'm a true believer that technology will change the landscape for the whole economy quite dramatically and for leadership." (Participant #20)
- "I suspect that if you draw a straight line, you would sort of see, you know, leadership style against the use of technology and it would sort of be version 1.0 style. But as you think about adopting more technology and you sort of democratize the information analysis available, you start thinking very differently about leadership." (Participant #10)
- "The fact that people have different expectations of leadership to some extent is also due to their access to technology. You can say that expectations of leaders will align themselves with the evolution of technology." (Participant #10)
- "Technology allows us to defy leadership. Before, we only had the newspaper and books. Now we have the powerful tools of social media, and leadership can be watched every minute, so leadership is far more exposed as well as leaders." (Participant #26)

- "The role of the leader is evolving because maybe they can be replaced with technology in the future. Both are merging." (Participant #28)

Networked Youth

Finally, Asian leaders noted that Asian youth was exerting pressure on society and organizations to move to more distributed leadership models. Participants noted how Millennials and Generation Z had arrived in the Asian workplace in large numbers with very different values and expectations of work and leadership. Millennials are defined by Nielsen Media Research (The Nielsen Company, 2018) as adults born between 1977 and 1995 and aged between 25 and 43 years old. Generation Z (Gen Z) is the demographic cohort succeeding Millennials born in the mid-to-late 1990s to the early 2010s. Both generations are technologically savvy and spend significant amounts of time on social networks, the internet (primarily from their mobile phone), and video and collaborative platforms. East Asia and Southeast Asia are the top two social markets worldwide, with US$1 billion in cumulative users accessing social media platforms across both regions (Kemp, 2016).

A highly networked younger generation was eager for more independence, access, and distributed leadership models:

- "The older generation Chinese are not international enough, even though they are very strong leaders, because they follow traditional leadership. But from my generation onwards, we're more internationally educated and connected by technology, and we have seen the Asian economic miracle giving us confidence and the humbleness to change leadership ways." (Participant #26)
- "A lot of Asian companies only were propelled through new wealth in the last decade or last two decades. So, you have the businessman in his 60s who is now passing on the company to his son or daughter, and that will change everything." (Participant #19)
- "When I was working in China, we would meet these old Chinese men in their 60s, and they were all caught up in their culture. But they understood they had to do something to bridge to us, and they brought the new generation of their children. They were brought up completely differently, understood technology, spoke English, and we could make deals with them at dinner without anyone losing face. The sons and daughters are the new leaders, and they know tomorrow will be different." (Expert #8)
- "I think it's even more challenging for Asian young people because obviously, they have a whole legacy, a set, a backdrop of how things were done; this is how your father has done things and how the organization

has been run this way. And now they have to transform the organization towards a more digital, a more transparent, a more engaged and communicative manner to integrate the best of the West and East." (Participant #19)

Consequently, participants explained that youth in Asia exhibited an "e-everything" mindset with expectations mirroring their use of technology: autonomy, transparency, open communication, and instant access to information. Youth from Gen Z believes in technology's promise to change everything, radically transforming organizations, eliminating hierarchy, and democratizing leadership. According to Asian leaders, youth look at jobs as a collection of experiences, using them as a portfolio approach to self-development. They are driven by learning rather than titles and salaries. Above all, youth have high expectations of leaders whom they see as mentors, exemplifying moral values and a strong "point of view" on the world. As a result, Millennials and Gen Z in Asia are driven by a sense of purpose with a desire for corporate leadership to address more substantial issues than corporate profit alone. They look to business leaders to tackle

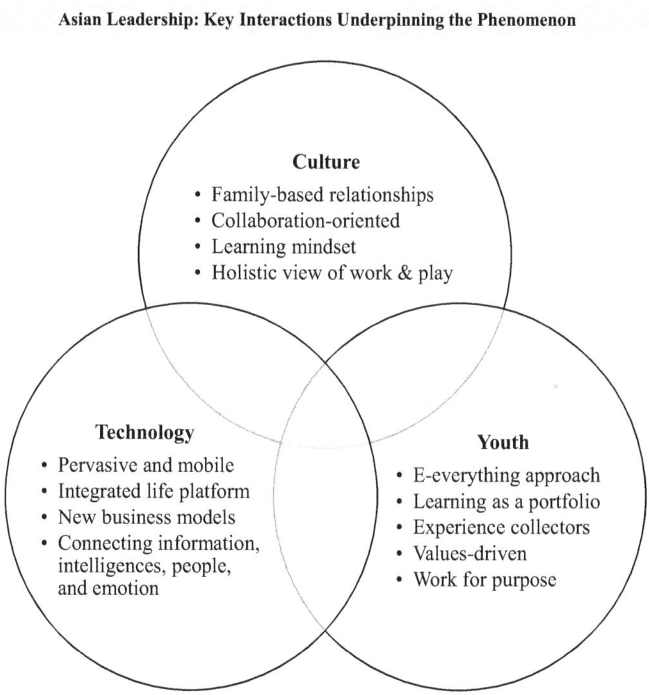

Figure 4.3 Asian Leadership: Key Interactions Underpinning Leadership Dynamics.

social justice, environmental issues, community engagement, and well-being through increased connectivity. This generational divide is putting significant pressure on leaders and how leadership is manifested.

In summary, Asia benefits from structural forces that favor a networked leadership approach (Figure 4.3). Aside from this unique cultural foundation, Asia exhibits other characteristics that prime it for more collective ways of leading. Youth and advanced networking technologies provide a new global setting where leadership has the potential to become more connected, distributed, follower-driven, crowd-based, networked, automated, and artificially generated. The evidence for understanding leadership as a participatory and digitally connected process is particularly compelling given the rapid evolution of technology, allowing collaborative learning, new forms of knowledge, engagement, and management. Asian leadership is rapidly morphing toward newer social norms to deliver on the aspirations of a younger workforce eager for more empowerment, community, and meaning.

References

Avolio, B. J., & Gardner, W. L. (2005). Authentic leadership development: Getting to the root of positive forms of leadership. *Leadership Quarterly*, *16*, 315–338. https://doi.org/10.1016/j.leaqua.2005.03.001

Bass, B. M. (1985). *Leadership and performance beyond expectation*. Free Press.

Blunt, P., & Jones, M. L. (1997). Exploring the limits of Western leadership theory in East Asia and Africa. *Personnel Review*, *26*(1/2), 6–23. https://doi.org/10.1108/00483489710157760

Bolman, L., & Deal, T. (2017). *Reframing organizations* (6th ed.). John Wiley & Sons.

Brown, M. E., Trevino, L., & Harrison, D. A. (2005). Ethical leadership: A social learning perspective for construct development and testing. *Organizational Behavior and Human Performance*, *97*, 117–134. https://doi.org/10.1016/j.obhdp.2005.03.002

Cashman, K. (1998). *Leadership from the inside out*. Executive Excellence Publishing.

Chen, H. Y., & Kao, H. S. R. (2009). Chinese paternalist leadership and non-Chinese subordinates' psychological health. *The International Journal of Human Resource Management*, *20*, 2533–2546. https://doi.org/10.1080/09585190903363839

Cheung, C., & Chan, A. C. (2008). Benefits of Hong Kong Chinese CEOs' Confucian and Daoist leadership styles. *Leadership and Organization Development Journal*, *29*, 474–503. https://doi.org/10.1108/01437730810894159

Collins, J. (2001). Level 5 leadership. The triumph of humility and fierce resolve. *Harvard Business Review*, *79*(1), 66–76. https://hbr.org/2001/01/level-5-leadership-the-triumph-of-humility-and-fierce-resolve-2

Dorfman, P., Javidan, M., Hanges, P., Dastmalchian, A., & House, R. (2012). GLOBE: A twenty year journey into the intriguing world of culture and leadership. *Journal of World Business*, *47*(4), 504–518. https://doi.org/10.1016/j.jwb.2012.01.004

Eagly, A. H. (2005). Achieving relational authenticity in leadership: Does gender matter? *Leadership Quarterly*, *16*, 459–474. https://doi.org/10.1016/j.leaqua.2005.03.007

Fry, L. W. (2003). Toward a theory of spiritual leadership. *The Leadership Quarterly*, *14*, 693–272. https://doi.org/10.1016/j.leaqua.2003.09.001

Fu, P. P., Wu, R., & Yang, Y. (2008). Chinese culture and leadership. In J. Chhokar, F. C. Brodbeck, & R. J. House (Eds.), *Culture and leadership across the world: The globe book of in-depth studies of 25 societies* (pp. 877–907). Taylor and Francis Group.

George, B., & Sims, P. (2007). *True north: Discover your authentic leadership* (1st ed.). John Wiley & Sons.

Goleman, D., Boyatzis, R., & McKee, A. (2013). *Primal leadership: Unleashing the power of emotional intelligence*. Harvard Business Review Press.

Hall, E. T. (1976). Beyond culture. *Anchor Press*. https://doi.org/10.2307/2064404

Hofstede, G. (1980). *Culture's consequences: International differences in work related values*. Sage Publishing.

Hofstede, G. (1991). Cultures and organizations: Software of the mind. *Development*, 1–29. http://westwood.wikispaces.com/file/view/Hofstede.pdf

Hofstede, G., Hofstede, G. J., & Minkov, M. (2010). *Cultures and organizations: Software of the mind, intercultural cooperation and its importance for survival* (3rd ed.). McGraw Hill.

House, R. J., Hanges, P. J., Javidan, M., Dorfman, P. W., & Gupta, V. (2004). *Culture, leadership, and organizations: The GLOBE study of 62 societies*. Sage Publications.

Inglehart, R., Haerpfer, C., Moreno, A., Welzel, C., Kizilova, K., Diez-Medrano, J., Lagos, M., Norris, P., Ponarin, E., & Puranen, B. (2014). *World values Survey: Wave 6 (2010–2014)*. http://www.worldvaluessurvey.org/images/Culture_Map_2017_conclusive.png

Inkeles, A., & Levinson, D. (1997). *National character: A psycho-social perspective*. Transaction Publishers.

Kemp, S. (2016). *Special reports: Digital in 2016*. We are social. https://wearesocial.com /special-reports/digital-in-2016

Kluckhohn, F. R., & Strodtbeck, F. L. (1961). *Variations in value orientations*. Peterson.

Li, J., Xin, K. R., Tsui, A. S., & Hambrick, D. C. (1999). Building effective international joint venture leadership teams in China. *Journal of World Business*, *34*, 52–68. https://doi.org/10.1016/S1090-9516(99)00007-3

Ling, W. (1989). Pattern of leadership behavior assessment in China. *Psychologia: An International Journal of Psychology in the Orient*, 32, 129–134.

Ling, W., & Fang, L. (2003). The Chinese leadership theory. In Mobley & Dorfman (Eds.), *Advances in global leadership* (pp. 183–204). Elsevier Science.

Ling, W., Long, C., & Deng, W. (1987). Construction of CPM scale for leadership behavior assessment. *Acta Psychologica Sinica*, *19*(2), 89–87. http://journal.psych.ac.cn/acps/EN/

McDonald, P. (2012). Confucian foundations to leadership: A study of Chinese business leaders across Greater China and South-East Asia. *Asia Pacific Business Review*, *8*(4), 465–487. https://doi.org/10.1080/13602381.2012.693770

The Nielsen Company. (2018, Fall). *Millennials on millennials*. The Nielsen Company. https://www.nielsen.com/wp-content/uploads/sites/3/2019/04/millennials-on-millennials-shopping-insights-report.pdf

Nisbett, R. E. (2004). *The geography of thought: How Asians and Westerners think differently and why*. Free Press.

Northouse, P. G. (2013). *Leadership: Theory and practice* (6th ed.). Sage Publishing.

Palmer, P. (2004). *A hidden wholeness: The journey toward an undivided life*. Jossey-Bass.

Rowley, C., & Ulrich, D. (2012). Introduction: Setting the scene for leadership in Asia. *Asia Pacific Business Review*, *18*(4), 451–463. https://doi.org/10.1080/13602381.2012.694726

Shamir, B., & Eilam, G. (2005). "What's your story?" A life-stories approach to authentic leadership development. *Leadership Quarterly*, 16, 395–417. https://doi.org/10.1016/j.leaqua.2005.03.005

Terry, R. W. (1993). *Authentic leadership: Courage in action*. Jossey-Bass.

Trompenaars, F., & Hampden-Turner, C. (1997). *Riding the waves of culture: Understanding cultural diversity in business* (2nd ed.). Nicholas Brealey Publishing.

Tsang, D. (2007). Leadership, national culture and performance management in the Chinese software industry. *International Journal of Productivity and Performance Management*, *5*, 270–284. https://doi.org/10.1108/17410400710745306

Ulrich, D., & Sutton, R. (2011). *Asian leadership: What works*. Ministry of Manpower Singapore. McGraw Hill.

Walumba, F. O., Avolio, B. J., Gardner, W. L., Wernsing, T. S., & Peterson, S. J. (2008). Authentic leadership: Development and validation of a theory-based measure. *Journal of Management*, *34*(1), 89–126. https://doi.org/10.1177/0149206307308913

Warner, M. (2010). In search of Confucian HRM: Theory and practice in greater China and beyond. *The International Journal of Human Resource Management*, *21*(12), 2053–2078. https://doi.org/10.1080/09585192.2010.509616

Wheatley, M. J. (1999). *Leadership and the new science: Discovering order in a chaotic world* (2nd ed.). Berrett-Koehler Publishers.

Zhou, Y., Kim, S., & Ru, D. (2019). Chivalrous idealist and pragmatic strategist: The influence of Mohist values on Ma Yun's leadership in China. *Asia Pacific Business Review*, *5*(2), 273–287. https://doi.org/10.1080/13602381.2018.1548546

5 Leadership Darwinism

Complexity, Disruption, and Uncertainty

Above and beyond the unique characteristics of Asian culture that encourage networked leadership, the global context of change has also compelled Asian leaders to evolve their ways of working and leading radically. Study participants and global leadership experts described a world in a deep state of flux, with 2020 marking a turning point of worldwide turmoil and instability. Disruption and uncertainty created what some participants described as a leadership vacuum and others called a full-on leadership "crisis." Experts tended to go further, indicating a regression of leadership into more authoritative and controlling approaches. This new environment was bringing out strong feelings of anxiety, anger, and mental health issues challenging leaders in entirely new ways and forcing them to get involved in many more personal and human resources issues than they were traditionally accustomed to.

Most noted that underlying structural conditions had been at work for decades (i.e., global order in flux, changing cultural norms, social injustice, the pace of change, technology disruption, and generational divide) and were compounding the leadership challenges leaders and teams experienced. When asked, "What challenges do leaders in the Asia region face when leading teams?" participants and experts first provided an overview of the rapidly evolving environmental context surrounding them, characterized by disruption.

The world was portrayed in a deep state of flux, with 2020 marking a turning point:

- "Everything changed within the last year; in fact, 2020 is really the date where people's understanding of the world and their part in it has changed; let's call it a thunderbolt year." (Participant #1)
- "This year is a deep spiritual and cultural reckoning for the world." (Participant #5)

DOI: 10.4324/9781003399377-11

- "I don't think ever before, there has been such pressure put on leadership." (Participant #7)
- "I don't think we will ever come back to normal again." (Participant #13)
- "You know, I think everyone in their heart wants to overcome this and get back to normal. But sometimes we know it may not be. Maybe we have to adjust to the new normal." (Participant #16)

Participants decried the global turmoil characterized by a global economic crisis, environmental disasters, gender issues, racial tensions, political instability, and social media distrust:

- "This is the first time in my life that I feel it's so critical to follow the news every morning. It's like a black swan every day. You just don't ever think about something like this would ever happen in your lifetime." (Participant #20)
- "Right now, the world is in such turmoil with the pandemic and what we have going on with all this social injustice and advocates and scholars who are speaking out." (Expert #1)
- "The world is facing some existential issues that for the first time in a couple of generations have forced us to actually consider our value system more deeply, like our environmental impact and diversity." (Expert #6)

The causal conditions for world disruption were twofold: (1) underlying structural conditions and (2) the recent global pandemic. First, participants and experts noted several factors that had been in motion for decades. The pace of change was accelerating:

- "How fast are you adapting to change? It's a constant question." (Participant #9)
- "There's no longer long-term planning. You cannot plan. It's changing all the time." (Participant #16)
- "The main challenge that we face is the team structure and the ways of working, which become obsolete every 6–12 months." (Participant #21)
- "Organizations need to be much more agile and flat in their decision-making. It's meant to be faster that way, right, to be able to respond to competitive threats or new trends that are happening faster, and it's not industry-specific; it's everywhere in the world." (Participant #22)
- "In the last 20 years, of course, the world has become far more disrupted. What's happened since then are two things: the world accelerated the way that business needed to move, and more agility was needed with a globalized world." (Expert #6)

Participants noted that technology disruption was a daily reality fostering change:

- "The disruption that technology has brought is huge, and it's happening across industry. So that is one huge leadership challenge." (Participant #9)
- "Technology and developers are changing things and the market so quickly." (Participant #11)
- "A big challenge that I'm facing is the digital transformation; it's a space that we're all trying to catch up in. The degree of understanding of the space is very different across different people." (Participant #28)
- "Many people have a very primitive understanding of what we mean by digital, so digital means different things to different people. If you are not embracing this kind of technology, then there's no way you can blossom and adapt to the change." (Participant #16)
- "AI and technology are really changing the world and challenging our former models of leadership." (Participant #25)
- "In the past, we didn't have such global connectivity. Now with technology, we express ourselves through so many online platforms, and there are more opinions. We now have to consider everyone's principles when leading." (Expert #1)

Social injustice was rampant based on wealth inequality:

- "The biggest problem globally is poverty, you know, the income gap, with rich people holding too much global wealth. So, the biggest challenge I will say for leadership is searching for a better society and solving the income gap." (Participant #26)
- "From a global perspective, I think there's a rise of social inequality with the haves and the have nots. And I believe that what I'm seeing is this groundswell of people who are saying, 'I'm going to do something. I'm going to take action because whoever is in charge is not taking action.'" (Expert #5)
- "I think there's been huge polarization whether you look at income or the distribution of wealth over the last 50 years. It's incredible. And that has created the grounds for people to gravitate to leadership with the stereotypical strong men, like Trump or Modi." (Expert #2)

Changing cultural norms were placing leadership at the heart of societal issues:

- "The whole world has a far-reaching impact on leadership, and multinational leaders need to be cognizant of not just generating profits. They need to care about the environment, care about the people, the community, and all that cultural sensitivity is even more important with all these geopolitical tensions." (Participant #19)

- "You haven't necessarily been schooled in that way of dealing with the world and dealing with people in a socio-psychological sense, nor do we have the right role models around us. The visible role models of leadership are very much retrograde. And so, the challenge that many leaders have faced over the last 20 years is to cede control, to let go of the reins to give people autonomy in order to facilitate happier, healthier organizations." (Expert #6)

The COVID-19 Shock

Aside from these deep structural conditions (i.e., global order in flux, changing cultural norms, social injustice, the pace of change, technology disruption, and generational divide), the global pandemic was seen as an unexpected shock of gigantic proportions, further aggravating the disruption in the world. Participants described COVID as a reset moment, raising questions on the very existence of life and economic activity:

- "I look at COVID as the great reset." (Expert #5)
- "Suddenly a small little organism that you can't even see to the naked eye has made the entire world shut down, adding to the problems we already had and creating a reset." (Participant #9)
- "I think it's been called the biggest test of courage and conviction." (Participant #14)
- "It's a moment you realize how vulnerable actually human beings are." (Participant #26)
- "Suddenly, people have seen how fragile humanity can be." (Participant #9)
- "It's called into question the very existence of the business and some industries; so, it's really, I think, stretched minds." (Participant #17)
- "COVID has been an inflection point with unintended consequences, remote working, work–life balance, the stock market, fear, what is essential and what isn't." (Expert #3)
- "The impact of COVID is gigantic; I really think it is a seminal shift; we're going to work differently, and we're going to need to lead differently." (Expert #6)

COVID-19 was seen as a change accelerator:

- "COVID has been a dividing moment and an accelerant to change." (Participant #13)
- "Satya Nadella said it right: it's been two years of transformation done in two months!" (Participant #12)

- "You would have heard from Satya, right: two years of transformation in two months." (Participant #15)
- "The behavior of social connectivity has been going on for at least five years, and COVID-19 has just accelerated it." (Participant #20)
- "COVID just accelerated the pace of transformation, and it has taught us to deal with a lot more ambiguity, fast and uncertain changes." (Participant #19)
- "COVID, oh, it's been huge. I think people are looking at this going, 'Oh my gosh, we have to accelerate our digital programs and digital transformation to step up because it's like, well, 'How do we continue to service our customers?'" (Expert #11)

Fundamentally, COVID-19 was interpreted as a test of leadership:

- "I think COVID is not a health crisis, to be honest. It's a deep crisis of leadership." (Participant #5)
- "It's been a crisis that has been telling. So, there are companies that talk about how core people are to them, but at the first sign of trouble, they're doing these massive layoffs. It's time to walk the talk. So, leadership has been tested." (Participant #23)
- "So, in my opinion, for leadership at this moment, nobody comes to mind. I cannot name a single leader around the world saying, 'Hey, this person knows how to get us out of this darkness.' A lot of the young generation has lost confidence and don't believe in leadership anymore. COVID made that clear." (Participant #26)
- "COVID is resetting leadership and how we're looking at it differently. It's made us question or made us have these discussions on how we develop leaders for the next generation." (Expert #5)
- "Now that we're in a recession, people need to be far more adaptable, and I think the need in leadership has turned into the type of model of adaptive leadership at speed, and that has very big implications for the individual because most individuals are not set up psychologically to cope with that and to deal with that world that we're living in now, a world where leadership is distributed." (Expert #6)
- "On leadership in general, I think people had to learn to accept that they have to live with a situation where their direct reports are not physically present. This is a big change for Asia, where the traditional way of managing is that the boss sits in front of a big room with all their staff there. So, it's probably been an even more serious shock in Asia because this idea of working from home or remotely is not so common. So now this COVID has forced everyone to change and be able to become like a startup almost." (Expert #12)

The widespread disruption characterizing the world was creating a new level of uncertainty that made Asian leaders feel they had to step up to address in new ways:

- "The world is a messy place, where so much is unknown and seemingly volatile and chaotic, it doesn't feel great to the average person." (Participant #3)
- "There's so much uncertainty right now that's happening everywhere in the world externally. The biggest challenge that I have is articulating my impact. I'm questioning myself, and I feel I have imposter syndrome. I don't have enough resources to create the impact that I'd like for the business right now." (Participant #28)
- "There's never been a scarier and more uncertain time." (Participant #14)
- "We are in a situation for which there's no reference to follow. You'll have to figure it out yourself. It's not something you have prepared for accurately with so much uncertainty, so you are off balance, and you have to follow your inner compass only." (Participant #26)

Participants described strong feelings of tension, mistrust, anxiety, anger, and injustice that they were personally experiencing and had to manage with their direct reports:

- "I personally have been outraged with everything going on." (Participant #5)
- "People are just looking at the world around them, and they see a lot of redundancies happening, 'What does that mean for me, my family, my work, my career?' It's all these unknowns that are creating anxiety." (Participant #18)
- "Many young people are living alone, so in this kind of an environment, to be alone and not be sure of whether tomorrow your job will go or will it remain, can be quite disturbing and harrowing." (Participant #9)
- "People's sense of what was normal, and things were taken away, and they're overwhelmed, and they're traumatized, and they're anxious." (Participant #5)
- Mental health problems were highlighted as a new leadership challenge:
- "My biggest challenge is my team's mental health." (Participant #5)
- "Some people are suffering mental health issues, and on the Zoom call, they look absolutely fine." (Participant #7)
- "Personal well-being is a top concern for leaders now." (Participant #13)
- "A lot of the youngsters are living on their own and suddenly find themselves tremendously in a sense of isolation, even though technology has enabled connectivity far better than before. Suddenly, now they're

having to cook for themselves and clean for themselves. There is fear of going out and not being able to distinguish work time and playtime by sitting at home. All this has created a sense of despondency, which can lead to depression if not tackled." (Participant #24)
- "A lot of people are sitting alone in their apartments. So, as leaders, we're going to need to attend to things that were far more hidden than in the past and will be much more visible in the future, namely mental health." (Expert #6))

Participants noted that the overwhelming sense of disruption and uncertainty equated to a crisis of leadership:

- "I don't think ever before, there has such pressure put on leadership." (Participant #7)
- "You know, it's an interesting time because to me, it feels like leadership is in a very transitional state right now." (Participant #25)
- "I'm a very different human being. I think there's a dearth of leadership, and people are outraged about the entire thing." (Participant #5)
- "I think basically there is a death of leadership." (Participant #19)
- "I think the responsibility of leadership is missing right now." (Participant #16)

Leadership experts tended to go further, indicating a potential regression of leadership into more authoritative and controlling approaches:

- "Leadership at a political level has gone back to the Middle Ages, in many ways, as if there is one individual who would know what to do all the time. It's a descent into authoritarianism. From a corporate side also, we seem to be gravitating more towards personalities, and narcissism is on the rise." (Expert #2)
- "The reality now politically is that people are taking back control and becoming far more autocratic in the way that they exhibit and demonstrate leadership. And I think, unfortunately, that some of that will naturally transfer into organizations because we use role models. I think we're going to end up with a struggle fairly soon in organizations where people will change back and say, 'Well, isn't it right that we should become more command and control again?'" (Expert #6)
- "There's been wider levels of fear and anxiety in society; people are worried about the future, about their place in the world, etc., and because of that worry and fear, the standard desire from people is to have the authority leadership." (Expert #13)
- "Look at the US, what's happening: there's a lack of leadership, I would say, from a government perspective. So, then you have these other leaders

rising up and saying, 'We need to do something,' whether that be state or be citizens rising up. This is really reshaping leadership." (Expert #5)

Participants and experts agreed that disruption and uncertainty had brought on an age of complexity for leadership:

- "Things are so complicated; there's just so much complexity." (Participant #13)
- "There's a lot more challenges and complexity as well." (Participant #8)
- "The kinds of challenges that we're facing today can't be solved by a single country, a single company or person because they're so complex." (Participant #22)
- "So, if I can describe leadership now versus in the past ten years, I would describe it now as being incredibly complex." (Expert #1)
- "The world is not getting easier today. The world is more difficult, more complex, more complicated for us." (Expert # 8)
- "Leadership is broader, a lot more encompassing, and it's to do with the world that we live in today. It's a lot more complex, a lot more uncertain, and corporates are expected to step up." (Participant #19)
- "The complexity of the problems, I think, is much more different and challenging for leadership. You know, before, as I said, leadership really was much more local, but now an election in the US has significant ramifications globally. Actually, an election in the Philippines has significant ramifications regionally, which in turn can have ramifications globally. So, there's this whole interconnectedness and this whole new complexity." (Participant #25)
- "I think the world needs a more collective style of leadership to solve these increasingly complex problems. And I don't think that one person with the loudest voice can do it." (Expert #5)
- "There's a lot of complexity, and when you're the CEO of a global firm with thousands of people around the world, you cannot manage the whole thing. So, there's been a necessity to delegate and operate in a world where teams are distributed, and organizations work in complex matrices." (Expert #6)

Generational Divide

Finally, a major structural issue faced by leaders was the generational divide, which was seen as particularly acute in Asia due to the youth of the population in most countries:

- "What's different is the workforce right now. Because if you look at all the demography of the population, especially in emerging markets, it's a young population. And sooner or later, the magnitude of the size of the Millennials who come into the workplace will become the majority workforce, and this is becoming a new norm for all leadership." (Participant #12)

- "There are multigenerational workforce pressures and managing the expectations of different groups of stakeholders." (Participant #27)
- "I think there's a generation gap because when the younger people come into the workplace, they have a different expectation of a leader, and you couldn't actually bridge that gap." (Participant #6)
- "The impact of young people on leadership is huge. Anyone born after 1996 has a very different view of leadership and a very different view of diversity and inclusion. And in Asia, you've got countries that have a very large population of young workers, right. So Vietnam, Indonesia, China, India. We also have Japan. Maybe not in such a large percentage, but you do have a significant shift happening in Japan with that younger group called the 'Satori' generation. They see the world differently and interact with technology differently." (Expert #5)
- "In the Indian context of hierarchy and privilege, they don't see why these younger people are becoming directors in three or five-year's time when it took them 20 years." (Participant #17)
- "There's a personal challenge and tension between the older generation and the younger one, but they have both a lot to learn from each other." (Participant #23)
- "What Millennials are doing is they're creating discomfort. I see it because some of the conversations I'm having with senior leaders, they invariably always come back to a kind of generational conflict. If you give Millennials an idea or a direction or an influence, they immediately start to challenge it, and that's changing leadership and creating a crisis of confidence in senior leaders." (Expert #4)

Millennials were seen to have different values and mindsets, such as autonomy, independence, and being quite outspoken due to their exposure to social media:

- "What is clearly a massive reason for change is the Millennial generation coming into the workforce, and with that comes a different mindset, different expectations of their career and their role in the world." (Participant #8)
- "I think Millennials today have grown up living through technology, and they're really quite independent, particularly like in China and Asia. They're basically from the one-child policy, and they're thinking how they want to do things the way they want." (Participant #11)

- "They're more exposed to media of different sorts and to technology that enables very democratic ways of working." (Participant #10)
- "The Millennials and young people are more aware of the issues of our times because of information access and their constant consumption of social media." (Expert #3)
- "We brought them up to have confidence, have autonomy, you know, to be able to question things, to be curious, so that's what they're doing, and it's challenging leaders." (Participant #6)
- "In Indian culture, often people don't speak up because of consensus. The younger guys are not afraid and are charged up with ideas. They have this sense of confidence and don't care about ruffling feathers." (Participant #23)
- "They are not achievement oriented like us. They want to express themselves, put videos on TikTok, be different, be recognized." (Participant #20)

As a result, Millennials' expectations of work and leadership were unique, requiring more communication and transparency and less hierarchy and control:

- "They've gotten different ways of expressing themselves and don't expect the same from the leadership. They expect you to communicate more and share where you're coming from." (Participant #14)
- "I think the Millennials have very different ideas about how to lead organizations, how to work, how to use social platforms. It's not just about one person holding on to a certain knowledge because there's a lot of transparency." (Participant #4)
- "Millennials want more transparency. They want to know, 'Why are we doing this, what's the ultimate goal?' to see the transparency from beginning to the end and how this leads to the bigger picture." (Expert #9)
- "Millennials want a sense of access. They want platforms and opportunities and leaders who make way for that. They want success early and to grow fast." (Participant #7)
- "Millennials would like to have access to the top management as an open-door policy and remove all the barriers of power of distance. It's super important to make sure they know that we as a leader don't exercise power of distance." (Participant #12)
- "There's a war for talent, and young people will not stay if you just tell them what to do. Take an MBA at 26 or 27 years old, and he or she will tolerate that kind of construct. You've got to be a little looser with your control structures and give people a bit more autonomy." (Expert #6)

Another characteristic noted by participants and experts was the youth's interest in societal issues, such as social injustice, the environment, and a search for a greater purpose:

- "We see the Millennials speaking out, especially about pride and social injustice." (Expert #1)
- "They actually want to work and be able to contribute to the survival of this planet." (Participant #6)
- "I think the expectation of younger talent is very different. They're looking way beyond salary, for other aspects around people, purpose, culture, a sense of pride when they're talking to their friends or individuals about the organization." (Participant #13)
- "When we look at the younger generation and the current workforce, they are very, very cautious about social justice. This will require leadership to really understand what exactly the purpose of the organization is rather than the P&L alone." (Participant #2)
- "Millennials have a different way of working. They want transformational leadership and purpose. Today, transformational leadership needs to really focus on the purpose, not on the task, because this young generation came into the workforce with the ability to use technology even faster." (Participant #12)
- "When you hire younger employees and Millennials, they ask much more questions about what the company is doing around the community, giving back to CSR programs, and the whole idea of purpose-driven organizations and all that. So that's the one trend that started maybe five years ago, and it has accelerated." (Participant #22)
- "Leadership to them possibly means really being recognized for doing something different. Not necessarily leading large teams, but maybe it's around working for a company that's more ethical or being part of a larger cause." (Participant #17)

As a result of all these differences, leaders confessed to not knowing what youth's trigger points were:

- "You have to be kind of cautious, knowing what motivates them. They want to be different. So, we have to be really smart to understand what would be the trigger with them, the community, and the environment. So, we can influence them." (Participant #11)
- "I think if I look at the number one challenge, it's how to work with the younger generation; it's a very purpose-driven generation. They can be very subjective. But the moment when they buy into something, they would just give their whole heart. So, I think the challenge for the leader is to identify what exactly is their trigger point." (Participant #2)

Leaders also expressed concerns about talent retention given the volatility of the younger generation and their lack of corporate loyalty:

- "We all know that they don't want to be routed to one place and work in a company for the next 15 years. That's all gone. There's a huge amount of restlessness. So, I think one big challenge for any leader is to figure out how you keep your best talent." (Participant #9)
- "Because talent churn exists to such a great degree, particularly in Asia, organizations are reluctant to put that long-term planning and investment into young people sometimes. They pop in and out of jobs and want to try many different things." (Participant #13)
- "They have financial security with their parents and grandparents as a safety net, so they can move from one job to another." (Participant #12)
- "Most of the evidence points to the fact that they are unlikely to be loyal to any one single organization." (Expert #6)

Asian leaders appeared to be on the cusp of fundamental secular changes, faced with a new age of complexity, the rise of tech-savvy Generation Z, and the emergence of novel, disruptive technologies. Participants and

Top Leadership Challenges	
Environmental	Pace of Change Business Survival Technology Disruption Uncertainty
Aims	Team Trust Individual Understanding Collective Empowerment
Process	Communication Bonding Humility Empathy Compassion
People	Generational Gap Talent Acquisition/retention Mental Health Diversity
Structure	Safe Environment
Measurement	Less Quantitative, More Qualitative

Figure 5.1 Summary of Top Leadership Challenges.

experts placed their challenges within a context of greater complexity characterized by disruption and uncertainty, resulting in a profound leadership transformation. Figure 5.1 summarizes the main leadership challenges that leaders in the Asia region faced when leading teams.

The culmination of these factors and the interplay between them is pivotal in understanding new leadership approaches emerging – why and how they have come to bear – and the Leadership Darwinism that Asian leaders are displaying in an effort to adjust to a world in flux.

6 Networked Leadership

Emerging Leadership Phenomenon

Asian leaders and their teams work, communicate, and connect in novel ways. They are displaying a new kind of mindset toward leadership, experimenting with new practices, and having higher aspirations for what teamwork can achieve. The result is a profound transformation of the role of leaders and those typically called "followers." Many of the changes outlined in the research are ground-breaking and challenge our accepted beliefs on what leadership typically looks like and how it is practiced.

"Leadership on a blockchain" describes how leaders and teams in Asia are shifting their understanding and practices of leadership from a process led primarily by an individual to a system of collective and digitally connected relationships. It is a concept and a descriptive account, lifted from the study participants' own words, that articulates an emerging leadership phenomenon. The metaphor provides a helpful frame to depict how leaders and teams operate. The expression also captures the logic of networked information technology to understand how leadership has transformed into a distributed and connected process. To present findings most compellingly to the reader and those less familiar with blockchain technology, the original themes of the research have been augmented with supplemental information on blockchain principles. Both the technical aspects of blockchain and its philosophical roots demonstrate the analogy's saliency and its innovative and informative construct to understand the new leadership dynamics at play.

Start-Up Culture

When asked, "What leadership approaches and paradigms (contrasting leader-centric versus team-centric) do you use in your day-to-day work?" research participants shared that they displayed a different kind of leadership mindset and novel ways of working. Asian leaders demonstrated high levels of adaptability to cope with the complex environment surrounding

DOI: 10.4324/9781003399377-12

them. Most participants described their way of working as some form of agile and adaptable process:

- "We collaborate very much in an agile-based approach with high velocity, high-frequency check-ins at the start of the day and at the end of the day." (Participant #8)
- "We are dynamic and agile because I think there's a managerial philosophy to pick the young stars to challenge them to grow fast." (Participant #20).
- "We're constantly moving, what they call now 'fail fast, fail forward,' you know, we follow a very iterative innovation approach within the company. So, it's not just with start-ups. We're all going flatter and more agile." (Participant #22)
- "Actually, a really interesting trend around agility and agile transformations is the talk in Asia about them. There's not a lot of organizations that are experimenting with it. So, what's happening is actually a lot of the leaders are being asked to lead these kinds of transformations, whether they be chief digital officers, or the CEO, or even the COO. But no matter what happens, they absolutely have to take other leaders on the transformation journey." (Expert #11)

They notably explained how they were breaking traditional ways of working and developing a start-up culture in their teams:

- "When I recruit people, 'I say, guys, we're doing a start-up, and you are the cofounders.'" (Participant #2)
- "My team is kind of like a start-up within a big Asian firm." (Participant #16)
- "We work like a start-up, culture is as flat as possible, not top-down. And it's okay to fail." (Participant #18)
- "We are a start-up culture, we experiment a lot, we are entrepreneurial, collective, faster, and messy. Work is essentially a big experiment for us." (Participant #29)
- "We work like a start-up because the only way you can grow is to relinquish control from the top and create many, many leaders." (Participant #24)

Transparency, Trust, and Democracy

Asian leaders were driven by core values of transparency and trust and sought to remove traditional signs of power, challenging hierarchical ways of working, and making leadership more democratic:

- "Here, power does not come from rank; it's based on the project you're leading. If you're leading Singles Day, you are the powerful one, sometimes even more powerful than the president of certain business units." (Participant #20)

- "I started to realize this whole thing of hierarchy top-down just does not work. It is a lot about understanding and recognizing the value that often people on the front lines and more junior level create, so we can improve ourselves. It's really about flipping the whole hierarchy over on its head." (Participant #27)
- "That's been a fantastic process to see around less hierarchy, relationships and giving people more of a voice." (Participant #3)
- "I make every decision very, very democratic." (Participant #7)
- "I would describe the working style as democratic. What's valued is a lot more your personal grit and determination and the hard work you bring to the table. It's very much more egalitarian. And I think this is looked at not just as a value to be spoken about, but to be lived and breathed." (Participant #23).
- "I think if COVID has taught us a lesson, it's that nobody has the right to the best ideas based on hierarchy. Ideas can literally come from anywhere. If you don't give access to the junior person, you will never know what you're missing out on." (Participant #14)
- "It's a flat team without hierarchy and mostly informal authority. Authority comes from knowledge, from connecting the dots, not seniority or age." (Participant #16)
- "I use a polygon model versus hierarchy. I am in the middle of the polygon, and I function as the enabler; I build capabilities. I don't make decisions for my team." (Participant #29)
- "It's all about teamwork. It's not a factory where things happen with a certain position. With team building, you need to have a set of people working very consistently together towards a certain objective. There is a certain level of consistency that is required in teamwork, and they need to build a very healthy respect for each other to constantly arrive at a solution and like-mindedness so that they click well together. It's not about hierarchy at all." (Participant #24)
- "I think the only way organizations can go into the future is if they prepare for collective intelligence in an organization. They have to unlearn the nasty habits of alpha leadership and hierarchy and even the idea of how we succeed in organizations. The scorecards are completely conditioned around winning." (Expert #4)

With this new mindset came new ways of working and organizing. Leaders explained how they were experimenting with new structures to adapt to change and break up traditional corporate silos:

- "It's taken me a while to break down silos so we could collaborate better within our team and with other units." (Participant #18)

- "We are breaking a lot of silos in the last 12–18 months; there's no legacy in how we work anymore. We just keep adapting." (Participant #2)
- "Our work teams are amorphous; I would say they expand and contract on demand. The organization is a little shapeless. The team takes the shape of the problem or the opportunity that we are solving." (Participant #7)

Expertise

Asian leaders stressed the importance of creating domain expertise within their teams using specialists:

- "No one really knows everything. And so, our team is structured in a way that people bring spikes of domain expertise." (Participant #8)
- "I think there's a recognition that to deliver an outstanding job for your organization, you need to rely on specialists, and you might have a particular area that you are an expert in, and you need to collaborate very effectively to deliver a solution that is rounded." (Participant #13)
- "The leader is like the maestro of an orchestra. You have to rely on having picked outstanding musicians who are experts in their instrument, playing the French horn or the saxophone, and trust everyone to do their part." (Participant #25)
- "You have to let go and bring in people who complement your skills because there's just so much to learn." (Participant #15)
- "We don't do things in isolation. We're quite conscious of the dynamics of interpersonal relationships, and there's a lot of respect because everyone brings their area of specialization." (Participant #4)
- "There's this discussion about everybody working up as a pool of talent, and you get roped into a project based on your expertise." (Participant #28)
- "I guess the organization will be a lot more productive if we can break up tasks, so there's more interdependence. It means the individual who does the task needs to have more domain expertise instead of people knowing a little bit of everything. Also, information that's needed can become shared equally across the organization instead of having to rely on someone to assess it." (Expert #9)

Specialists were also brought on as part-time or project workers:

- "I hire interns more than my full-time employees because I want to facilitate a change culture and having specialists, especially in digital." (Participant #12)
- "Today, the way the world is moving and where resources are all over the world, you need to access people from different parts of the globe on a long- and short-term basis." (Participant #24)

- "When it comes to short-term projects like a pitch, we work in coalitions. It's not like teamwork; you don't need to know people's strengths; you don't need to like me. I can just come into the room; I can solve your problem as an expert and leave, and that's a coalition. So, what is happening in today's business is a mix of both more teamwork and coalitions depending on the type of project we work on." (Participant #24)
- "I have to be prepared to be leading an organization where not everyone is in my formal team structure, and I need to learn how to make them purposeful and productive when they are part of it. The reality is that I don't see the future where everyone is a full-time employee in your team; you're going to have a team structure where a bunch of them are going to be gig contributors who are coming in for a specific project or for a specific thing that needs to get done." (Participant #27)
- "Knowledge can be distributed in a network that is not located in a single place. The one example is flying an airplane from New York to Paris; no one person has that knowledge." (Expert #10)

Growth Mindset

To facilitate the development of special capabilities and skills, leaders described how they were developing a culture of constant learning:

- "I think of our organization like being a learning organism. It takes the best bits of everything and evolves." (Participant #8)
- "It's no longer a know-it-all mentality. It's about creating a learning mentality." (Participant #15)
- "You need to encourage a growth mindset." (Participant #17)
- "It's really important to always be curious and keep learning, have that growth mindset." (Participant #18)
- "We do a lot of internal education and external sessions to learn and groom our people." (Participant #13)
- "We select new leaders based on learning and a trial process. We keep good HR records, and we have a scoring system to track people based on their projects. Each person gets to lead a bigger project with learning, so there's a laddering process from a leadership and project management standpoint. Leadership is like a trial process versus ranking." (Participant #20)
- "The boundaries or the context in which people are learning is widening. It's what we call 'learning in the wild.' We start to notice that learning and knowledge processes in organizations are integrated into aspects of daily activities in the organization. Professionals are engaged

through daily activities to advance their knowledge. We see open practices of learning and innovation. So, from a leadership point of view, it's important to create this open space for facilitation of learning and knowledge processes; you could say that the boundaries of organizations are sort of unfolding and sort of opening up." (Expert #7)

Team Collaboration

Collaboration was the pervasive way of working in teams:

- "Collaboration becomes absolutely critical because of the complexity." (Participant #13)
- "A lot of leaders talk about divide and rule. They like to create a kind of healthy competition. But what we realized is that building collaboration with each other is a better strategy than a sense of competition between teams. It gives people faith and trust instead of building silos. It's a visual image of holding hands with each other for fighting whatever is coming." (Participant #7)
- "Collaboration is a very strong value we hold, and that guides our way of working." (Participant #29)
- "Our team is very, very collaborative. It's a very homey culture; everyone takes care of each other quite a bit." (Participant #17)

Technology was relied on heavily for team collaboration and used by the leaders themselves to keep up with their teams:

- "It's a collective leadership model where everybody has access to the decision-making process enabled by technology." (Expert #4)
- "The way we collaborate is simply through technology everywhere: video, Google Docs. Just click, and you're responsible, and you can assign any action to someone. I would say the analogy is that technology is like our coffee." (Participant #12)
- "When I was at Twitter, I had responsibility for Latin American markets, Middle East, North Africa countries in Asia. I didn't visit for a year and a half or two years at a time, and I still led those people. So, it was a form of leadership that was radically different; e-leadership, I think is possible, and using technology to be a remote leader." (Participant #3)
- "It's how you build those interpersonal skills using virtual leadership. You cannot do that without technology and especially video. When I arrived in my new job, we didn't even have video conferencing. I could not see my team, so I ended up getting a personal Zoom account." (Participant #22)

To facilitate collaboration, leaders noted how they were investing heavily in communication with their teams, often describing it as a necessary "overcommunication" approach:

- "Leaders are overinvesting their time to communicate and connect and just speak to people and just being there for them and recognizing how difficult it is for people personally and professionally right now." (Participant #13)
- "Our trust level has gone up because we're actually overcommunicating." (Participant #19)
- "We over-communicate to support and do regular check-ins, just to make sure the teams do have a sense of belonging, empowerment, and trust." (Participant #11)
- "We have realized the importance of communication; I would say even the need to overcommunicate." (Participant #14)
- "We all know we need to overcommunicate. In times of crisis, it's not too much, 'Hey, how are you doing? Are you okay? Do you need help?' As simple as that." (Participant #15)

Informal communication channels (i.e., team huddles, stand-ups, instant messages, virtual chats, and online coffees) were becoming more popular for teamwork, sometimes displacing formal channels:

- "So, we're really upping the ante in terms of trying to increase the number of calls and check-in sessions, so employees get to hear from the leaders instead of the formal quarterly town hall. We're starting to do smaller informal bite-sized chunks of communications." (Participant #19)
- "We use informal channels like our team WhatsApp group." (Participant #8)
- "It is very important that as a leader you are not waiting for the formal channels of communication to inform you about what is important and where value is being created." (Participant #27)
- "We have a company WhatsApp group. But, you know, we would use it to post each other on business, and it's now become also sort of like the underground subversive communication process for chatting and gossiping." (Participant #25)
- "In our weekly stand-up, we don't talk about business performance; it's more about bonding and getting to know each other, which has helped immensely. It's that social connection. Last month, I gave a class on cooking." (Participant #18)
- "So, we do town halls every three months for major announcements. But we've also created smaller groups to create more interactivity. There's a bunch of youngsters who started something called the Culture

Club to do music, karaoke, stand-up comedy, cooking, just to connect." (Participant #24)

Distributed Leadership

At the heart of the new ways of working was the distribution of leadership through shared decision-making and collective influence:

- "I feel a lot of the decision-making and the power is in the team, and they are empowered to come up with the decisions and ideas themselves." (Participant #10)
- "You have to be as transparent as possible to give confidence to everyone and let them make the decisions." (Participant #18)
- "Leadership is a bit like a blockchain. It's a comparison where leadership becomes distributed, not the prerogative of one person because this person has more degrees or more knowledge, but it's about plurality and making the best use of, you know, the different qualities and different capabilities within teams and optimizing that. And so, I think, yeah, it just becomes more distributed, and we just rotate in terms of leadership." (Participant #4)
- "There's a lot of that transparency and shared knowledge, and people are able to take on leadership roles regardless of what your job title is." (Participant #4)
- "Our way of working is very project-based. We only manage under the project management philosophy, so we assign a project, project members task force on that, and so the leadership happens, day in and day out within a group, so everybody can be leaders, and it depends on what project you're leading." (Participant #20)
- "We use the DARCI model when working. We use it to identify the right leader depending on who is the subject matter for each project. Everyone can become a leader as a result." (Participant #29)
- "We share leadership. Different people play the lead at different times to make the project successful. Our founder said that 'the three of us together are bigger than each of us.'" (Participant #24)
- "In certain situations, you may not be the leader. You may have to be very comfortable with letting go. And, you know, at least in American businesses, letting go is not something that a lot of companies are comfortable with." (Participant #25)
- "Distributed or shared leadership sits very nicely with the idea of networks and how knowledge and other processes are shaped and happening within these networks, and if you as a leader, if you feed those networks to flourish, then I think you will have a lot more power within your organization." (Expert #7)

Leaders challenged their teams to take on more accountability and ownership to share decisions together:

- "Nowadays, because people have more access to information, there's more knowledge across the team. So, the leader must empower the team to kind of inspire them to be more self-driven. It's more important than before." (Participant #11)
- "I don't give them the solution; it's more about giving them open questions versus tasks and let them find the answer themselves, so they have ownership to drive that solution on their own." (Participant #11)
- "We're not going to give you a list of things to do. We're going to give you an idea of where we want to go, but you, as the individual, need to figure out how to get there. Now that was a very big shift, and it takes a lot of coaching and confidence because the education system in Indonesia primes people for the fact that you're not allowed to fail." (Participant #21)
- "I give my team that ownership, 'Okay, look, I'm empowering, I'm trusting you, go and do it.'" (Participant #18)
- "I give a lot of freedom to my team; I invite them to co-create with each other and assume ownership to make things happen and own their decisions." (Participant #28)
- "From a leadership point of view, we should facilitate the process of autonomy and accountability. If you think about it from a knowledge practice or a knowledge ecology point of view, I think it's much wiser to make sure that you let people connect because if you give people lots of autonomy, they'll probably learn a lot and they also need to take up the responsibility to feed it back into the organization, so they bring the knowledge back." (Expert #7)

In summary, the leadership approaches described by Asian leaders were based on breaking traditional ways of working for

- High adaptability
- Domain expertise
- Distribution of leadership
- Team collaboration
- Relying heavily on networking approaches
- Using pervasive technology.

The mindset, values, and behaviors all supported a shift away from the traditional heroic leader-centric paradigm in favor of networked leadership.

Blockchain Principles

Why has this new leadership phenomenon been described as "leadership on a blockchain"? Let us take a step back to define blockchain technology and its principles. Blockchain is an innovative system of recording information for the digital age. As Zheng Fan, Executive Director of Higher Education at the Forbes Technology Council, explains, the technology is called a "blockchain" because it is comprised of a chain of blocks or "packages" of information wrapped up with data. Each block can store up to 1 MB of data, or about 4,000 transactions (Fan, 2019). Blockchain uses a network of distributed computers to record data. The information recorded can be tangible (i.e., a house, car, money, land) or intangible (i.e., intellectual property, patents, copyrights, branding). Blockchain functions as a public, decentralized, and distributed digital ledger; thus, it has enabled digital money in the form of cryptocurrency, among other things.

Through its innovative, disruptive technology, blockchain carries unique ethical components on information sharing, its users, and society at large. According to Galati (2018), "aside from its technological component, blockchain was fundamentally a political idea, attracting followers among libertarian and anarchist groups who saw in distributed systems the power of removing control from the grasping hands of governments." As a collection of philosophies and movements, libertarians uphold liberty as a core principle and aim to maximize political freedom and autonomy. As a decentralized, peer-to-peer, distributed system, blockchain's fundamental backbone elements are linked to rejecting authority and promoting individuality and freedom as core values. "I fit into the Web3 ideology, which is quirky, transparent, authentic, and [about] empathy," says Imgesu Cetin, 26, cofounder of Defy Trends (Klein, 2022).

The ideological elements of blockchain are also notable in Satoshi Nakamoto's whitepaper on Bitcoin, a peer-to-peer electronic cash system running on blockchain technology. Nakamoto explains that the motive for creating Bitcoin was dissatisfaction with the current financial system and mistrust toward financial actors and the Central Bank (Nakamoto, 2008). The idea was to create a purely peer-to-peer version of electronic cash that would allow online payments to be sent directly from one party to another without going through a financial institution. This method would offer a new global decentralized monetary system bypassing financial institutions that have served as the only trusted third parties to process electronic payments.

The design and architecture of blockchain build a distributed decentralized system where users, potentially located on different sides of the world, can interact and collaborate seamlessly. Blockchain aims to create a trusted, unfilterable, un-censorable repository of data and information accessible worldwide. Blockchain seeks to allow digital information to be recorded and distributed, but not edited. The technology makes it impossible to change, hack, delete, or cheat the system because the data is duplicated and distributed across the entire network of computer systems. Altering information retroactively would require the alteration of all subsequent blocks and the consensus of the network. "Blockchain has a decentralization nature as it runs on a distributed peer-to-peer network of computers (known as nodes) adhering to predefined consensus rules for validating transactions and adding blocks to the chain" (Fan, 2019). Therefore, a blockchain system can agree on a common truth without trusting a single machine or authority but the blocks of data in the chain themselves. In other words, the network can reach a consensus without an intermediary, higher authority, or leader figure. According to Rustie Lin, the Blockchain team education lead at Berkeley, "Instead of trusting the execution of individual processes or reliability of any individuals, we trust the general protocol and the math behind it. It's trust – without trust" (Lin, 2022).

More than a technology, blockchain can be considered an ideological experiment challenging the source, direction, and nature of power and authority, much like the new Asian leadership movement I uncovered. In peer-to-peer networks, peers partition tasks and share their computational power with other participants in the network. As a result, there is no need for any central coordination as the networks function based on (1) self-organization, (2) symmetric communication, and (3) distributed control. With networked leadership, there is a similar desire to rely on (1) self-organization via peer-to-peer collaboration, team member expertise, and empowerment; (2) symmetric communication through transparency, trust, and frequent communication, and (3) distributed control by distributing and sharing leadership.

While blockchain technology is still in its infancy stage with many new applications forthcoming (i.e., Web3 metaverse, non-fungible tokens (NFTs), smart contracts), the aim of the metaphor of "leadership on a blockchain" is to reflect upon the similar motivations and ways of working of the technology as those described by my research participants. Figure 6.1 provides a comparative view of Asian leadership and blockchain principles.

"Leadership on a blockchain" helps to stimulate an intellectual reflection on leadership by exploring new ideologies, philosophical motivations, and alternatives to the power imbalance typically held by a central authority and those who are ruled by it. The overarching idea of networked leadership and how it has been described and practiced in Asia is that centralization of power is destructive and ill-equipped to answer today's business,

Comparative View of Asian Leadership and Blockchain Principles

		Leadership	Blockchain
Paradigm	**Mindset**	Adaptability Agility Start-up culture	Disruptive Renegade Libertarian
	Core Values	Transparency Trust Democracy Empowerment	Authenticity Trust Freedom Autonomy
Ways of Working	**Specialized**	Domain Experts Specialists / Part-timers Always-on learning	Chain of blocks Packages of unique data
	Distributed	Scattered connected teams	Disparate connected computers
	Decentralized	Shared leadership Collective influence Informal	Self-organization Predefined consensus algorithms Anonymized
	Collaborative	Team-centric Technology-enabled Communications heavy	Peer-to-peer Network consensus Symmetric communication
	Networked	Teams Connected community	Connected nodes Shared computational power

Figure 6.1 Comparative View of Asian Leadership and Blockchain Principles.

human, and societal challenges. It aims to create a system without a central authority while still being able to regulate itself through network actors and provide advantages to those willing to take part in it. The hope is that it will guarantee its participants a new level of autonomy, agency, trust, and shared purpose.

References

Fan, Z. (2019, November 21). *Blockchain explained in plain English*. Linkedin. https://www.linkedin.com/pulse/blockchain-explained-plain-english-zheng-fan/

Galati, F. (2018, March 26). *Blockchain as a process: Ideologies and motivations behind the technology*. The Domino. https://medium.com/the-domino/blockchain-as-a-process-ideologies-and-motivations-behind-the-technology-c25219d87881

Klein, J. (2022, June 6). *The only woman at the ICO*. Elle. https://www.elle.com/culture/a39974691/the-women-of-crypto-june-2022/

Lin, R. (2022). *Blockchain technology* [Education Video]. Distributed Systems, Berkeley. https://courses.edx.org

Nakamoto, S. (2008, October 31) *Bitcoin: A peer-to-peer electronic cash system*. Bitcoin.org. https://bitcoin.org/bitcoin.pdf

Part II
Conclusion

Conclusion

Asia is uniquely placed to become a leadership sandbox of the future. Aspects of Asian culture have created a fertile soil for networked leadership: the holism of Asian thought; the importance of personal and professional networks in driving success; the importance of relationships, collective orientation, and harmony; individual integration within the social system of the family and community; pervasive use of technology; and a highly networked youth. Furthermore, Asian leaders have changed their leadership approaches, exercising a form of "Leadership Darwinism" to adapt to new macroeconomic, social, and technological changes.

As a result, Asian leaders are enacting "leadership on a blockchain," a new form of networked leadership that relies on start-up culture, a democratic approach to work, promoting transparency and trust, hiring, and connecting domain experts; enabling team collaboration; and distributing leadership through their networks. Blockchain principles provide a new lens to understand the motivations and solutions Asian leaders and their teams display for addressing twenty-first-century challenges.

These research findings are distilled into key lessons for global leaders in the upcoming Part 3 so practitioners can be agents of change and apply the learnings in their organizational setting.

DOI: 10.4324/9781003399377-13

Part III

Lessons for Global Leaders

Part III
Introduction

Introduction

Having laid out the "new geography of leadership" (Part 1) and presented how Asia is uniquely placed to become the leadership sandbox of the future (Part 2), it is now pertinent to ask what lessons global leaders can draw from these learnings (Part 3). How has the concept of leadership radically evolved? How can practitioners accelerate their leadership transformation? What company tools, processes, and structures can be developed to keep pace with technological innovation and disruption?

To answer these questions, a summary of leadership's inflection points in the last decade is presented with a "from–to" analysis contrasting the evolution of the business environment, changes in leadership goals, processes, relationships, structure, and measurement approaches. Participants verbatim illustrate the profound changes they are experiencing. The ideas articulated also come with new leadership language directly lifted from the research study's interviews to describe new relationships and dynamics between so-called "leaders" and "followers." A leadership manifesto for the digital age is offered alongside a reflection on the future of leadership. Finally, a practitioner's starter kit is provided with a new set of questions leaders and their teams can ask to implement a different approach to leadership.

DOI: 10.4324/9781003399377-15

7 An Evolving Leadership Construct

Leadership's Marked Inflection Points in the Last Decade

When asked to contrast leadership ten years ago versus today, participants and experts presented evidence of a profound leadership transformation (see Figure 7.1):

Leadership Evolution At A Glance

	Leadership 10 Years Ago	Leadership Today
Context	Stable	Unpredictable
	Hard Power	Soft Power
	Autocracy	Democracy
	Inherited	Earned
Aims	Profit-driven	Values-driven
	Prestige	Purpose
	Knowing	Learning
Process	Directing	Connecting
	Transactional	Transformational
	Task-oriented	Team-oriented
Relationships	Male-dominated	Diverse
	Individually driven	Collectively driven
	Managing shareholders	Managing multi-faced stakeholders
	Seniority	Ageless
	Position	Creation
	Fear/distance	Trust/proximity
	Force	Kindness
	IQ	EQ
	Organization-centric	Customer-centric
Structure	Hierarchy	Networks & Communities
	Top-down	Multi-directional
	Long lasting	Agile & Responsive
Measurement	Business KPIs/Metrics	Doing Good

Figure 7.1 Leadership Evolution at a Glance.

DOI: 10.4324/9781003399377-16

- "The difference between leadership ten years ago and today is black and white." (Participant #1)
- "I don't believe for the last nine years, things changed very much at all, and then everything changed." (Participant #1)
- "Ten years ago, it was a lot more smooth sailing for lack of a better word. I felt that leadership was a lot more seamless back then." (Expert #1)

Toward an Earned, Democratic, and Soft Power Approach to Leadership

First, the context of leadership changed from a relatively stable environment to a context of unpredictability:

- "Leadership used to be structured, safe, monotonous, unified, and one way." (Participant #29)
- "Today, the speed of change is unpredictable, and leadership has to answer to that." (Participant #13)

Soft power had become more critical than hard power:

- "There's a different kind of role model where it's not the usual mold. It's a different form of power. New leaders are not born rich or with a name like Rockefeller or Vanderbilt or whatever. They have soft power, using emotion." (Participant #5)
- "I think definitely the soft goals to me have become more important." (Participant #6)
- "I think those skills are a lot softer and a lot less autocratic than perhaps what they used to be." (Participant #13)
- "There's a lot more emphasis, I think, on the softer skills." (Participant #22)
- "Encouraging people, you know, the soft skills will be so much more in demand than they ever were." (Participant #9)
- "There is more emphasis on the softer side because intuitively, you know that people feel a bit more isolated than before. So, you need to make sure you build community and make yourself even more available as a leader." (Participant #14)
- "There's more effort on the softer issues, getting people comfortable with each other, getting them to open up, speak their minds a lot more, inviting the opinions of the group." (Participant #24)
- "Power today is about listening, making an impact, being responsible, role modeling, and taking the organization with you." (Participant #20)

The context of leadership shifted from autocracy to democracy:

- "It feels like good leaders have become much less autocratic in their style and much less dictatorial, 'I'm the boss, you will do this.' It has to be a lot more collaborative and supportive nowadays." (Participant #13)
- "Today, I would say that there is more distributed and democratic accountability with leaders." (Participant #7)
- "A leader used to be an autocrat, not anymore. Employees, especially Millennials, want to be heard, and they want to be recognized. They want to be part of things, not just take instructions, and want to play a meaningful role." (Participant #19)
- "Companies like Alibaba are trying to adopt a more distributed power approach, and therefore, I think a lot more peer-to-peer leadership, not just top-down leadership. I think that is actually very much what resonates with the core of Asian values and culture." (Participant #14)
- Leadership as a concept of power was seen as having evolved from being inherited to needing to be earned:
- "Leadership used to be very top driven and quite unaccountable, I would say because, I mean, if you're a leader, you kept all the cards very close to your chest." (Participant #7)
- "True leaders are those who've earned it nowadays. You earn the respect, the autonomy, the equity, the influence." (Participant #5)
- "Leaders today need to actually first and foremost be able to earn trust." (Participant #6)
- "A leader does not come with a rank. What matters to me is the qualities of the leadership, and the person has to prove it." (Participant #6)

Values-Driven and Purposeful Leadership

Aside from the changed context of leadership, participants noted that the aims of leadership had also altered. While leadership used to be entirely profit-driven in business, participants indicated that contemporary leadership was more values-driven:

- "Work was definitely a functional role many years ago. I don't think people talked about work satisfaction as much as we do now. I would say the narrative started changing about getting satisfaction at work, fulfillment, and values." (Participant #6)
- "For leaders, it was always about profits. Now suddenly, leaders are realizing, 'What do we do for the planet?' Now I need to balance citizenship and the social conduct of my company with the need for profits." (Expert #2)

- "Of course, profit is absolutely fundamental, but CEOs need to work out the correlation between positive movements, let's call it social and virtuous cycles, and the balance sheet. It requires a different mindset and a different way to look at the business and the organization." (Participant #1)

Leadership evolved from being about prestige to purpose:

- "New leaders want to win the hearts and minds of people. It's about purpose, whereas with the previous generation, it was essentially about money and the survival instinct." (Participant #19)
- "We are talking about leadership with purpose." (Participant #2)
- "It needs to be much more purpose-driven than perhaps it was ten years ago. I think leaders need to define a genuine purpose for their organization that can unify their teams." (Participant #13)
- "Young people are looking for leadership, someway, somehow, and government leaders are not giving it to them. So, they're looking elsewhere and for corporate leaders to essentially step up and take charge and demonstrate that strong leadership is there and that it can be done through the purpose of their own organization and impact the rest of the community around them." (Participant #19)
- "Leadership used to be guided by structure and systems; now it's driven by purpose." (Participant #29)
- Leadership was no longer about concentrating knowledge but distributing it and encouraging learning for self and others:
- "You know, 30 years ago, if you were in a senior leadership position, the expectation was that you were the smartest person in the room, and it was about you holding on to that knowledge." (Participant #25)
- "There's a lot of demand these days for people in leadership roles to actually be constantly learning, especially on the technology front." (Participant #6)

Team Bonding and Connection

The leadership process was altered dramatically. Leadership was no longer defined through directing subordinates but rather by connecting with people:

- "Earlier, leadership used to be, I mean, although it was never my style, you could have that style of a little dictatorial directing approach." (Participant #9)
- "It was still very much the strong man leadership approach and sort of the chain of command." (Participant #12)

- "If you talked to a leader 20 years ago, he would have said, 'I have my people in the office, and we have a task to do, and I keep an eye on everybody. And then we leave at 5:30 pm, and we go home, and then I begin my other life.' I think what's happening now is that there is no other life; everything is connected and integrated. You will be thinking about your people, and it may well be a globally distributed team who are communicating with you via a number of different channels all the time, even on the weekend, and there's a symbiosis and constant connection." (Expert #6)

Leadership was less transactional and task-oriented and more transformational and team-oriented:

- "It used to be about assigning roles, goals, and deadlines." (Participant #6)
- "Leaders would communicate in an almost like one-track way down to employees, and it was the law of instruction." (Participant #19)
- "Now people want the leader to be a bit more human, not just transactional or functional." (Participant #6)
- "People want the opportunity to be empowered, to actually go to a place where I otherwise wouldn't go without the leader." (Participant #6)

Relationship-Based Leadership

Overall, current leadership values reciprocal relationships and aims to be inclusive. The types of relationships characterizing leadership changed from being primarily male-dominated to being more diverse:

- "A leader needed to be a strong man, somebody who could get into a room and was a fighter." (Participant #27)
- "In India, it was extremely rare to see women in leadership positions. The lack of role models ten years ago was staggering. So, I think that's changing, and now you see many more women sit on the leadership team here in India." (Participant #23)
- "I think there is much more appreciation of diversity, not just of gender, but also the kind of skills that you bring to the table." (Participant #23)
- "I believe the number one challenge right now that CEOs are facing is the issue of diversity and inclusion. We need to make the boardroom more diverse and how we are ensuring that there are different types of representatives from all different cultures and backgrounds and ethnicities and skillsets." (Expert #1)

While leadership relationships used to be primarily driven by a solo individual, they had become increasingly collectively driven:

- "The archetype of the leader at the top of the pyramid, or at the front of the pack, whatever analogy you want to use; that's gone." (Participant #10)
- "Ten years ago, it was hierarchical, and they still saw the leader as that figurehead, and they followed the master way." (Participant #16)
- "We used to talk about big leaders, this person, and this person. Now that we're connected with technology, we realize leaders can be anyone. They don't need huge power as long as they're a force together." (Participant #26)

A decade back, leadership was primarily concerned with relationships with shareholders, while, today, participants described the importance of managing multifaceted stakeholders:

- "I think ten years ago it was only about charting the company's vision. It was only about operating profitably and answering to the shareholders." (Participant #19)
- "There is a conversation on the fact that as a business, we're in business for more than just money; we truly impact the lives of stakeholders at large in society." (Participant #17)
- "Today, it's a multifaceted group of stakeholders that the leaders need to answer to. No longer just to shareholders; you have to answer to staff, to the external community, partners, vendors, the government, activist groups." (Participant #19)
- "I think we're shifting from what is the purpose of an organization that used to create value for shareholders, all the way to the purpose of an organization to create value for a broader set of stakeholders." (Participant #10)

The face of leadership was no longer based on seniority or age:

- "We're starting to see that leaders can be young, and yet they can galvanize the world. Because being a leader today is about creating change because you've earned it or because you were affected by it. You can use emotion to galvanize, and you don't necessarily have to wait 30 years to be the boss suddenly." (Participant #5)
- "Young people, they just come out of nowhere, they prove that they can do well, be leaders and disrupt the entire way of things." (Participant #16)

Leadership was no longer a matter of position:

- "It's no longer because you're the boss that I listen to you. It has to be about an exchange of value, not rank." (Participant #16)
- "So, we've been moving for the last 40 years into flatter organizational structures, fewer hierarchies, and greater distributed teams and distributed leadership. And leadership within that isn't a position; it becomes an activity that's pushed to the edges of the organization." (Expert Interview #13)
- "I think historically there was more a cult of the leader. Whereas now it's the cult of the creator, no matter what position you have." (Participant #13)
- The fear, distance, and force built into leadership for decades were replaced by trust, proximity, and kindness:
- "There was definitively an element of ruling by fear. Today, that wouldn't cut it." (Participant #6)
- "Ten years ago, people saw a leader as kind of a role model, but you would feel a certain distance. But, today, I feel a leader is next to you all the time. You can consult with them and reach out to them. There's just a level of trust." (Participant #11)
- "I think that the strong leaders that stand out from this will be able to command the trust and the love of their staff. It will not be a style that's won through dictatorship; it's really a style that's won through the fusion of success with others." (Participant #19)
- "There's a stronger sense of mutual respect and trust between employees, independent of power relationship." (Participant #3)
- "Kindness now is hugely important." (Participant #9)
- "It's about leading with heart and the mind." (Participant #15)

Emotional intelligence and customer-centricity were described as very significant relationship dimensions for contemporary leadership:

- "I think it's become much more around EQ than IQ; it's a real sense of emotional intelligence and understanding of what people need personally and professionally." (Participant #13)
- "Effective leaders have to really demonstrate emotional intelligence and really understand their people and what motivates them, and you know their strengths and their weaknesses." (Participant #13)
- "Leadership EQ is more important now than it was earlier." (Participant #9)
- "Everything needs to start with the EQ and translate down to the customer." (Participant #1)
- "All businesses have to respond to much more demanding employees and customers, and so leaders need to have higher EQ." (Participant #14)

Networks and Communities

The structure of leadership evolved from hierarchical to networks:

- "Before it was all about hierarchy. Now I think people want to be treated as another decent human being. People want to be treated like you know they're actually able to think and get respect." (Participant #6)
- "Well, I think one of the things I'd say from my experience is how the hierarchies of before no longer exist. Cheryl Sandberg talked about it how it's not a career ladder anymore but a jungle gym. Your willingness to go up, down, sideways in your career is essential." (Participant #22)
- "I think organizational structures have changed. They used to be the classic top-down structure hierarchy. Now it's more like a jazz band playing together where everyone improvises." (Participant #24)
- "It's not about the people who report to you; it's about the people in your network that you can influence." (Participant #22)
- "In the past, organizations were very ordered and directed; it was high command and control. Now, organizations are actually described in terms of what a neuroscientist would say is like neural networks." (Participant #25)

Leadership structures were becoming more agile and responsive to change:

- "The speed of change is creating organizational structures that need to be agile and where you can react and hire individuals who are prepared to respond." (Participant #13)
- "It's about the pace of change and how you anticipate that change so that you can evolve with agility. It's about building a very dynamic and agile workforce culture that can shift very quickly." (Participant #10)
- "You have to change the way you work and the way you make decisions to be a lot more agile. And so, I think that presents itself as a very clear business challenge." (Participant #14)

What Counts: Doing Well and Doing Good

Finally, participants and experts noted that leadership was measured differently, shifting from less tangible metrics to more qualitative forms of evaluation:

- "The Baby Boomer leadership style is really KPI centric and a reward and punishment style." (Participant #12)
- "Leadership used to be all the things you could measure, the tangible stuff." (Participant #6)

- "Performance metrics were heavily weighted on financials, and you know, they were easily measured because of their numbers; it would be fairly straightforward. Now there are trade-offs that could be financial, against people, against the community, the environment, and all these different things. And you know it's very difficult optimizing every single one of them." (Participant #10)
- "You don't just decide on your performance goals anymore. You actually have to take in the feedback from the ground up in terms of what your employees want, what they care for, and what's good for the community." (Participant #19)
- "Ten years ago, the CEO was just trying to put together a team to help run the company and to meet organizational outcomes and goals. Now, there are so many different factors a CEO has to consider." (Expert #1)
- "Is your company building the world or destroying the world?" (Participant #5)
- "Today's leadership evaluation is, 'Are you a force for good?" (Participant #1)

In summary, the evolution of leadership over the last decade was dramatic – it presents a significant transformation not just in the way that leaders and teams are working but also in how they are building relationships, the nature of the goals they aim to achieve, and how they plan to measure leadership outcomes.

Leadership Through Connectivity and Purpose

The Leadership Connection: Humility, Vulnerability, Compassion, and Empathy

Asian leaders described how they were moving away from directive leadership in favor of facilitation. They also shared how they were becoming more people-focused and developing a new level of connectivity with their teams:

- "The leader becomes more of a facilitator rather than keep the direction or make all the decisions; it's more a process of facilitation." (Participant #2)
- "The leader is just a facilitator, really." (Participant #4)

Leadership, as participants enacted it, was based on creating and growing connections to

- Connect information across the organization, thus democratizing leadership through learning and equal information access

- Connect people to tasks by identifying and matching domain expertise areas to projects
- Connect various forms of intelligence to create better solutions and outcomes
- Connect people for human bonding, emotion, and collective energy.

Asian leaders depicted themselves as "connectors" and the "glue" between others, seeking to be in constant connection with their teams, even outside of work, and taking time to manage an extended network of relationships both inside and outside the organization. When describing how to mentor and grow other leaders, Asian leaders did not discuss training for individual leadership competencies but rather encouraged the formation of networks and relationships. Connection skills were deemed essential for leadership success. This connectivity was based on demonstrating emotional intelligence and the ability to nurture people:

- "I don't want to sound cliché, but my role is first about people." (Participant #18)
- "In Chinese, we say, 'You need to cultivate the heart first.'" (Participant #26)
- "The organizational change I'm doing right now is looking for people with different forms of intelligence: IQ, EQ, AQ (I made that one up, it's their Adversity Quotient), and DQ, the Decency Quotient, 'Are you a decent leader and a good human being?'" (Participant #5)
- "I think that the emotional intelligence piece is critical. The way that then it affects leadership and hiring organizational practices if done well has really significant impact and ramifications throughout an organization." (Participant #13)
- "What the leader needs to do today is spend extra hours to nurture; that's what leading really means." (Participant #12)
- "You need compassion and to be able to listen and to be able to talk about stuff outside of the office, to be able to nurture, make friends with your people a little more. All that has become especially important in the post-COVID world." (Participant #9)

Leaders also discussed the importance of humility for leadership today:

- "There's a lot more recognition of humility. I feel humility wasn't really part of the toolkit of leaders before. But I think there's a recognition that you as the leader don't know it all." (Participant #17)
- "With the impact of technology, you suddenly see a lot of people in very senior positions realizing that they need to catch up on some of the skillsets, and therefore they become a lot more humble, open to learning new things, and not embarrassed to ask questions. There's a recognition

that just because you work in an industry for a long time, you don't have all the answers." (Participant #28)

- "A lot more humble and really bringing people with them on a journey as opposed to, 'I'm the big boss, you'll do what I say.'" (Participant #13)
- "Be highly communicative and very humble, willing to take feedback, willing to take advice." (Participant #19)
- "There is an urgent need for constructive humility to make up for the glorification of individuals and a heavy dose of arrogance in leadership at the moment. Humility becomes a very valuable commodity because it percolates down and becomes a character of an organization, and that can have spillover benefits." (Expert #2)

In addition, Asian leaders explained how they were demonstrating more vulnerability and compassion toward their teams:

- "So, I think that's the transition which is happening in leadership now: people are open and much more vulnerable." (Participant #23)
- "People want that authenticity, you know, emotions, which used to have no room in the boardroom. Now, if you're not authentic, you cannot lead. And vulnerability that's become a number one superpower, particularly in Asia." (Participant #5)
- "You have to show your vulnerability because you have to admit what you don't know." (Participant #15)
- "The COVID effect is going to last for some time, and in certain cases, there might be permanent changes that should be taking place. So, therefore, leadership has to be compassionate." (Participant #9)
- "What's happening in the world takes a toll emotionally on people, and therefore, I think that compassionate leadership or a leadership that listens to more than just your rational problems and becomes your emotional guide is needed more and more." (Participant #9)
- "People want compassionate leadership, I mean fundamentally it's about, 'Do you care about my me?'" (Participant #18)
- "In the past, I think leadership qualities were defined by the alpha male, but I think there are intrinsic female qualities like compassion and having more empathy and having more EQ that matter now." (Participant #4)
- "I think a leader has to be more open, very personal, and compassionate so people can feel that they can tell you what they're struggling with. It's typically not something that is natural for some of the male leaders because it reveals a bit more of the personal or the emotional side. We need leaders that are more empathetic, more caring, more nurturing." (Participant #22)

Collaboration was driven by a deep sense of empathy for team members:

- "So, whether you're letting go of people or you're motivating people, you know employee experiences are in the limelight like never before. So, the leader has to be empathetic, be much more thoughtful and considerate than ever before, because it has huge ramifications." (Participant #17)
- "I think having a sense of empathy is very important. We're putting ourselves into our team's shoes when we communicate with them. I think that's the difference culturally." (Participant #11)
- "Leaders need to have empathy because without that, how can you understand others and their basic needs, or someone who is working remotely or in a different language? So that's really where I see the biggest change from before." (Participant #15)
- "Empathy; it's almost like a unique signature that I have. I'm extremely people-oriented." (Participant #17)
- "It's about being able to have a lot of empathy for the people who are involved in that process. And this COVID situation has brought out the reality that leaders need to understand their context and therefore develop empathy that can go with that." (Participant #27)
- "COVID has meant that leaders need to be more constructive and have empathy." (Expert #2)
- "With COVID, I guess the leader has to show more empathy because the circumstances are more stressful. So, you need to be more empathetic, and when things are slower moving, less efficient, more mistakes are made or whatever, I would discount that stress." (Expert #9)
- "Companies have to lead, manage, and work virtually and determine how to look at globally distributed teams. We help leaders build capacity around things like empathy and have meaningful conversations with people at a time when there's so much overwhelming stress." (Expert #11)

Asian leaders were demonstrating emotional intelligence (Goleman, 1998) and moral virtues of "empathy," "humility," "compassion," and "vulnerability," as previously highlighted in the Asian leadership literature (see Part 2). The Chinese CPM leadership behavioral model (Ling et al., 1987) advances that a leader's character (the "C" factor) is a critical leadership competency that confers the right of the leader to play a more prominent role in society. Similarly, the Chinese implicit leadership theory (Ling, 1989) identifies personal morality as the top-ranked dimension of Chinese leadership, noting that personal morality is a critical cultural expectation of leadership. Alibaba's former CEO, Jack Ma (2018), an iconic global Chinese leader, spoke about the evolution of leadership, noting that "last century, people competed with muscle. This century, it's not muscle; it's wisdom." He stressed the importance of having high EQ for success, even noting the importance of "LQ," the Love Intelligence Quotient.

Purposeful Leadership: Justice, Equity, and Diversity

Aside from developing a new level of connectivity with their teams, Asian leaders also explained that purpose was a net new factor in their leadership considerations. It was cited as one of the main reasons explaining the way leadership was enacted in Asia because of societal and cultural expectations, new expectations of Asian youth in the workplace, and team motivation. Participants and experts agreed that leadership had become more anchored on purpose, with a growing concern for justice – leadership for good was accelerating.

Participants' search for purpose was also motivated by a more significant collective endeavor to provide a sense of direction to business activity and the meaning of life. Teams aspired to be driven by a higher purpose beyond merely sharing work commitments:

- "When you find yourself being a leader, you need to chart a bigger purpose, bigger than yourself, to make other people's lives better or the world." (Participant #26)
- "Purpose is the fundamental thing. It's almost like that NorthStar of what your company believes in and what leaders are all about." (Participant #19)
- "When you are a leader, people are looking up to you. They don't just want somebody to show them the way but also what that person stands for, what does he believe in, does he support A versus B, you know, what are his world views on society, what is the purpose?" (Participant #9)
- "I'm a connector; I believe in bringing people along. Our success is a collective success, harnessing the strength of everyone for a shared purpose." (Participant #15)
- "I would say we begin with defining what the broader purpose is of what we want to achieve." (Participant #15)
- "My role as a leader is making sure everyone in the organization understands why we are doing this and why it's so important, giving people a shared purpose." (Participant #12)
- "Leaders cannot follow a value system that is just a motto written on the gateway of the lobby anymore. They have to walk the talk and make their teams live the values. In Chinese, we say, 'The pearl is threaded.'" (Participant #20)

Ethical concerns, diversity, and inclusion were essential values in driving teams:

- "I think the world has been calling for a particular kind of leadership; I don't like the word, but I'm going to use it; it's ethical leadership with a concern for society and the world." (Participant #5)
- "Before, people were not as conscious or careful about making sure that everybody was consulted, or that everybody felt included, but now it is important to make sure that people are included." (Participant #4)
- "I think teams nowadays are a lot more diverse; they have different teams composed of people from different backgrounds, ethnicities, and a lot more diversity from all different parts of the world." (Expert #1)
- "We need diversity because if you want to serve the world, you have to represent the world." (Participant #15).
- "When all the knowledge becomes available to everyone, then diversity becomes an important quality of a team." (Participant #4)

The Changing Roles of Leaders and Followers

Participants and experts outlined significant implications resulting from the leadership transformation: (1) the changing role of leaders from providing direction to facilitation, (2) the changing role of followers from gaining alignment to providing domain expertise, and (3) the changing role of organizations, moving from seeking employee commitment to manifesting a greater purpose. The transformation of leadership, the role of leaders, followers, and their shared goals are summarized in Figure 7.2.

Followers as Co-founders and Teachers

The changing roles of leaders and followers were underscored by the new leadership language proposed by the study participants. For example, the word "followers" was seen as inadequate and antiquated:

- "The word 'followers…' I wouldn't necessarily call them that. I actually see them as leaders in their own right. Especially when you work with the younger generation, they don't see themselves as followers at all." (Participant #19)
- "The idea of followers needs to be retired because one thing that happened is that the key to leadership is not just somebody who shows me the way, but leadership is someone who gives me confidence, who brings out the best in me and gives me room to fly so I can lead too." (Participant #9)

Past versus Present: Summary of Leadership Entities and Outcomes

Entity	**Outcome**		
	Past		Present
Leaders	Direction	→	Facilitation
Followers	Alignment	→	Domain Expertise
Shared Goals	Commitment	→	Purpose

Figure 7.2 Past Versus Present: Summary of Leadership Entities and Outcomes.

Source: Adapted from Rosenhead et al. (2019, p. 12, Table 9). Complexity theory and leadership practice: A review, a critique, and some recommendations. *Leadership Quarterly*, *30*(5). https://doi.org/10.1016/j.leaqua.2019.07.002

- "So, it's interesting that I am a little bit uncomfortable with the word 'followers.' I feel like, as a leader, you need to have the ability to build a community. I feel like when you have followers, they just follow you. You don't get something back. Whereas I feel like in my experience, being a leader, I actually get a lot more from my team, right? It's almost like I impart things to them, but they also bring things back to me." (Participant #24)
- "To me, 'followers' connotes the kind of people who are behind you. But another way to think about it is that I wouldn't really say that people are necessarily followers, right, but they're just part of the leadership team." (Participant #10)
- "I don't see my people as followers. I would describe them as leaders. The leader–follower hierarchy is a misconception." (Participant #29)
- "The idea of the superhero who can step in and save the day and somehow patronize the follower and steer; let's get away from that language of influence. I think we need a new model of leadership that moves away from transformational language and even moves away from the language of 'leader and follower,' and we can get more into a different kind of language around collaboration integration and collectivism." (Expert #4)

Participants used new language to describe followers as "co-founders," "backers," "passengers," and "teachers":

- "There are no followers; they are my co-founders' team and back me up." (Participant #2)
- "We have shared values, and we back each other up. The whole idea is that people stand up for each other right, and there's a sense of coverage that can come from anyone." (Participant #7)
- "Followers have become journeymen and women, passengers that go with you, not follow you." (Participant #9)
- "The youngest people and most junior people in the room are the ones that are more digitally native and give the seniors the input because they're out of their depth. So, the followers are the new teachers." (Participant #28)

Leaders as Relationship Brokers and Mobilizers

As followers were increasingly seen as leaders in their own right, the role of leaders was also redefined. Most notably, participants indicated that leaders were no longer the central source of knowledge:

- "Historically, a leader might have had authority on the basis that they had more information or more knowledge. You look towards a leader because the leader knows everything. But in an era where you have access to a lot more information and knowledge, and sometimes because you might even know more about a particular field or domain than your leader, then it is no longer about the fact that the leader has knowledge or superiority." (Participant #10)
- "You know, 30 years ago, if you were in a senior leadership position, the expectation was that you were the smartest person in the room. You had done the job because you were the expert. Fast forward to today, with the explosion of knowledge and information. There's no way the leader can know everything." (Participant #25)
- "So, the traditional leadership, right, I would say, maybe in the 70s, you would expect the leader to actually know everything, right? The person sets the direction and makes sure that they are the fixer of the basic mission and so forth. But in this world, you're facing more ambiguity, and leaders don't know it all." (Participant #15)
- "The leader is not expected to know everything and have the utmost decision-making power. It's not about holding that knowledge anymore but being able to find the best-qualified people." (Participant #4)

- "One thing I know for sure is that I don't know everything. My role as a leader is to be a participant and a learner." (Participant #8)
- "Everybody's got access now, so I need a leader who tells me how I can learn things. Earlier, you looked up to the leader because they were the best and knew more than you, not anymore." (Participant #9)
- "I think leaders need to recognize that you don't always have the best idea. You have to create an effect on the rest of the organization so that everyone feels they have a role to play to contribute to a better outcome for the company." (Participant #14)
- "I would like to think that all leaders know that they're not the smartest person in the room. If we can get to a place where, as a leader, you know that your job is to bring this diverse group of people to address whatever that problem might be." (Participant #22)

As a result, many leaders talked about the importance of dispensing with the ego traditionally associated with leadership:

- "Leaders who have big egos will not cut it anymore; you have to be part of a work team." (Participant #2)
- "There needs to be a removal of ego to lead today." (Participant #5)
- "Leadership has to restructure itself by letting go of ego." (Participant #26)
- "Leadership should not be about catering to the ego of the leader, which is very tempting. What you should do as a leader is rather coordinate, get in the right mode to understand which expertise is demanded, at what point of time, and then bring the right person in." (Expert #8)
- "I would describe the change as: from the sage on the stage to the guide to the side. It's a paradigm that relates to learning with the teacher on the podium lecturing for knowledge transfer, as opposed to the teacher as the facilitator of group learning processes." (Expert #7)

As facilitators, leaders were focused on creating the right environment for their teams:

- "It's not necessarily about, okay, the leader's vision. I mean, of course, those things are important, but also to create an environment that is safe for people to feel like they can express themselves and can do things collectively. It's what is really changing everything because then you see that the team forms beautifully into sort of a community." (Participant #28)
- "Right now, my leadership role is to create the environment, and my role is to give them nurturing." (Participant #16)
- "I think what's really important for me is to create an environment that helps facilitate collaboration and inspires that creativity." (Participant #18)

- "It comes down to building an environment for your colleagues, your teams, your employees in order to produce the best type of work that's needed to move the company forward." (Participant #21)
- "Leaders, your job is not to score the goal. You just need to be the best midfielder in the business. Someone else will score the goal, but you've got to make it so easy, extend that generosity, create that space, giving it to someone to score." (Participant #24)
- "If you are leading an organization with all these networks that you're trying to empower, what you do is rather than sort of delegate, now you provide the space." (Expert #7)
- "So, in my book, I use the term 'swarm leadership.' The beekeeper is, for me, the person who creates the environment; it can create the condition and emergence. That person that can come from any place in the structure and can begin to have the conversations to create the environment for people to have a more collective experience." (Expert #4)

Leaders acted as brokers of relationships, alternating between being "advocates," "coaches," and "mobilizers":

- "When I work within the vertical line of my company, I am an advocate. I help my team understand the corporate strategy and what it means to them short and long term and mobilize our resources to get there. I'm facilitating that envisioning process as well as on top of my personal advocacy if it's not clear. On the horizontal line (aka within my team), I'm a relationship broker, and I manage people, their roles on projects, and spotting who can be the next leader. I'm almost doing human resource allocation." (Participant #20)
- "I'm more like a connector. I'm the one who connects this team to the rest of the organization, pretty much in terms of resourcing and information flow. I'm flexing it as a leader." (Participant #23)
- "My leadership is fluid, from knowing when to intervene to knowing when to only check in with the team. It requires a certain amount of wisdom, perspectives, and self-awareness." (Participant #27)
- "I speak last. I listen more. I make my role a supportive role; I am more of a coach." (Participant #29)
- "People don't just do what we tell them. I'm the coach, and my team are the leaders, in fact." (Participant #29).

The fundamental role of leaders was to act as "connectors" – not just of information but of people and emotion:

- "I see my role as empowerment, connecting, and enablement. I would say I'm a connecting enablement person, and in doing so, it allows my team to have a platform." (Participant #8)

- "Connecting people is the world's most important proposition." (Participant #1)
- "My main area of expertise is managing people, and the second is really connecting that because there are so many things moving around, so I have to be the one being accountable to connect the dots." (Participant #11)
- "Leadership must be about a form of connecting knowledge with and through others." (Expert #4)

Leaders demonstrated a new aptitude – the ability to mobilize and energize others:

- "I don't call myself a CEO, I call myself a Chief Energy Officer. I need my people energized and driven to a purpose." (Participant #7)
- "It's not about the leader making decisions on behalf of the group, but it's about somebody who can get that momentum going with the group so they can actually make a change of decision together." (Participant #4)
- "I see the leader's role as increasingly as a curator, a mobilizer of people through a sequence of interconnected people, actions, enablers, and stakeholders." (Participant #10).
- "The leader is a catalyst. It's about harnessing energy because it's something that doesn't have a limitation, whereas time is limited. Therefore, you need to be a lot more balanced in all aspects of your life, creating the synergy between people and then blending together life and work in a way that is giving momentum, energy within the team." (Participant #28)
- "Catalyzing people's energy to a purpose has been our greatest way of working and giving a huge amount of warmth and personal touch in realizing it." (Participant #7)
- "If we're talking trends, today the literature would be the literature of caring, the duty of care. Care, connect, and contribute." (Expert #10)

Experts explained that leadership with connection and purpose departed from traditional, centralized aims and control mechanisms, leading to new emergent outcomes:

- "Well, as soon as they come out with a mission statement and things like that, I roll my eyes; that's the old way of running an organization. To my mind, the new way of running an organization is respecting that individuals have their own values, their own aspirations and that they are working toward those and trying to find ways of creating mechanisms of cooperation that are fulfilling their objectives, which leads to an emergent result." (Expert #10)

- "I don't dismiss the idea around having some form of organization. I just think that we need to organize it in a different way, as long as a goal is not a conditioning goal but is an agreed and shared goal." (Expert #4)
- "A network is a perceptual system. What will emerge from a network depends on what it perceives. So possibly a leader modeling and or demonstrating collaboration might be a role that creates emergence." (Expert #10)

Finally, participants and experts discussed the changing role of organizations, moving toward network structures.

- "Every business is basically becoming a technology business and a network business." (Participant #13)
- "Your company can survive in the shared economy only with decentralized professional networking, but you can't just become a platform but a company that makes sense for society through networks." (Participant #20)
- "I believe that a structure that facilitates conditioning is against forms of collective intelligence. Take honeybees: they have clear roles, they go off, they will do sense-making, they will scan, they will build intelligence, and they will come back, they will begin to work with a colony with these levels of intelligence. They will filter it down, and then they will make a group decision. And I think we're in a good place to do that with leadership, given the technology that's coming through." (Expert #4)

In conclusion, leadership approaches and paradigms used by Asian leaders and their teams were team-centric, in marked contrast to leader-centric approaches. Asian leaders noted the changing nature of leadership based on greater connectivity and purpose. Participants and experts outlined changes at three levels: (1) the changing role of followers becoming leaders in their own right; (2) the changing role of leaders as connectors of information, people, and emotion; and (3) the changing role of organizations, moving toward network structures, letting go of centralized aims and control mechanisms in favor of new emergent outcomes.

References

Goleman, D. (1998). *Working with emotional intelligence*. Bantam Books.
Ling, W. (1989). Pattern of leadership behavior assessment in China. *Psychologia: An International Journal of Psychology in the Orient*, 32, 129–134.

Ling, W., Long, C., & Deng, W. (1987). Construction of CPM scale for leadership behavior assessment. *Acta Psychologica Sinica*, *19*(2), 89–87. http://journal.psych.ac.cn/acps/EN/

Ma, J. (2018). *Jack Ma: Love is important in business, Davos 2018*. World Economic Forum. https://www.youtube.com/watch?v=4zzVjonyHcQ

Rosenhead, J., Franco, L. A., Grint, K., & Friedland, B. (2019). Complexity theory and leadership practice: A review, a critique, and some recommendations. *Leadership Quarterly*, *30*(5). https://doi.org/10.1016/j.leaqua.2019.07.002

8 Leadership Manifesto for the Digital Age

As parting thoughts, study participants and experts were asked to reflect on the future of leadership in Asia and suggest a book title that could capture the profound changes they witnessed. They considered several aspects, including the importance of creating a new understanding of leadership, codifying a new leadership process, exercising new practices, and having clarity on a new end game for leadership.

A New Understanding of Leadership

Overall, participants had a positive outlook for leadership and saw an opportunity for substantial renewal in the future:

- "Well, I actually look at the future very positively." (Participant #1)
- "Yeah, I'm hopeful, we're moving in the right direction; it's just not that fast, although we have all the tools and technology already." (Participant #3)
- "We will always need leadership in the future because leadership matters; it's just going to be something very different." (Participant #20)

Participants and experts agreed that it was a pivotal time for leadership as they were entering "a new leadership era" manifested by new awareness and mental models:

- "I'd like to think that we are going into, for lack of a better word, almost like a new era, whereby we're seeking some form of enlightenment." (Participant #6)
- "I think we're going to have to raise the level of awareness of what leadership really is. We need a new level of consciousness, actually. I think most leaders are not fit for purpose. In order to lead effectively in this new world, I think we need to become deeply grounded in ourselves first." (Expert #6)

DOI: 10.4324/9781003399377-17

- "In the past, leadership had a very sharp silhouette, you know, you had a very sharp idea in mind of what was a leader, but now it's very blurred lines. I would hope to see some new leadership models emerge." (Participant #16)
- "We've always started the whole leadership conversation with the sort of classic ID of the leader; you know, it's an older man with a beard, he sort of looks very strong and powerful and all these kinds of things. That is so deficient, and we need to facilitate a transformation of letting go. I don't think we have that image yet; we haven't created it culturally. It needs to be softer and visualize allies by giving your power away. I like the opportunity to think about how we can create a new icon for leadership to foster new understanding." (Expert #7)

Global leadership experts were more cautious than Asian leaders, noting that the opportunity for leadership reinvention might take longer and face obstacles given the current global crisis of leadership and the lack of role models in public life. One global leadership expert chose to title his book on the future of leadership: "Purpose, chaos, and navigating uncertainty" (Expert #5).

New Leadership Practices

Research findings evidenced that leadership practices were shifting from concentrated (leader-centric) to distributed (team-enabled). Suggested book titles on the future of leadership included:

- "Democratizing leadership." (Participant #3)
- "Representative leadership." (Participant #3)
- "From Hierarchy to Merit." (Participant #5)
- "Leading from the center of the polygon." (Participant #29)
- "The future of us." (Participant #27)
- "The death of Superman and the birth of the Avengers." (Expert #13)
- "Leadership as a blockchain." (Participant #4)

Participants situated the future of leadership in a post-heroic leadership paradigm in line with the changes they were already undertaking as leaders in their teams:

- "In the future, leadership will be a lot more distributed. We will be leading from the passenger seat, and purpose will be the driver, not the person anymore." (Participant #29)

- "I think it's all about democratizing leadership, where distributed people take turns leading." (Participant #4)
- "We went from the corner office to the open office, which democratized work, and then came COVID, and there's no office anymore! So, what it means for leadership is that we went from leadership charisma, personality, and physical presence to a new human emotional structure." (Participant #9)
- "I guess you could finally go all the way to the end of the spectrum, which is, you know, everyone's a leader." (Participant #10)
- "The best leaders will be able to lead without knowing because they will be open to actually being led themselves." (Participant #6)

Both groups were eager to chart changes, starting with the need to evolve to new organizational structures supporting new leadership models:

- "I think we should stop the conversation around leadership transformation. And I think we should have more conversations around organizational behavior and digital transformation. We have to change the actual organization in terms of the whole system and the sort of technology enabler for that." (Expert #4)
- "Leadership is becoming more like organized organizational environment design." (Expert #10)
- "I think design skills are going to be super critical in the future. Leaders will have to design different organizational structures." (Participant #3)

Less centralized models based on collaboration were seen as the way of the future:

- "I think that what will happen is that organizations will get flat. I think there will be a lot of specialists who are working together rather than having very hierarchical organizations." (Participant #23)
- "Leadership will keep evolving. I think employees are going to be more fluid because you can work for this company now and then go and work for this company then. And you're going to see a lot of fluidity in the workforce, and that actually impacts leadership." (Expert #5)
- "In 20 years, you won't be working for a company. You'll actually have seven or eight resources or swarms you'll be working for, and you'll be connected to those through technology. Everything will be connected, and I won't see employees or workers or followers; what I see is real resources pulled into a swarm decision-making process." (Expert #4)

Participants also pointed out the importance of promoting new ways of hiring (based on values more than just skills) and developing new kinds of leaders:

- "Our business schools that do these leadership programs are churning out the leaders of tomorrow. How do we make sure that they're building into the curriculum and into the educational system new ideas that challenge the stereotypes that follow certain frameworks, like 'strong men'?" (Participant #22)
- "What's depressing for me is that we're teaching these tools, particularly to younger leaders and the mid-level, which are about categorization and these approaches around influencing and control, working the hierarchy, gaining commitment, and the rest. I think none of this will be relevant in probably even ten years. It's actually counterproductive and dangerous to the whole collective intelligence." (Expert #4)
- "I think leadership development is going to be more of a systems thinking, more expansive than focused on the individual as is typically the case in US firms and their frameworks." (Expert #5)

New Leadership Process

Research findings revealed the importance of treating the leadership process as a form of deep human connection rather than a transactional process. Participants proposed book titles, including:

- "Don't follow me; walk with me; we'll go together." (Participant #9)
- "The connector curator leadership approach." (Participant #10)
- "Shining the light on others and illuminating the way together." (Participant #17)
- "The leadership murmuration." (Participant #25)

Participants saw leadership evolving toward social and psychological sciences rather than merely business management, with the leader embracing a key connector role frequently referred to as the team "glue":

- "I think a good leader of a team within an organization needs to create purpose and bond with collaboration. Provide togetherness and a glue without potentially much physical contact." (Participant #13)
- "Leaders should not be the boss, be the glue. Bosses provide authoritarian hierarchy, whereas being the glue is what holds a team together." (Participant #24)
- "The leader is really the glue for everything together, bringing knowledge together and the right talent. Leadership should be circles of

influence: one element is creating influence around you, and then there's a circle for the team, and then a bigger circle of influence of leading the organization through change. It's all interconnected." (Participant #11)
- "The level of power distance between leaders and employees will shift substantially. I think that ultimately people will self-organize, and the concept of leadership will be much more about how you build great teams of people that believe in what they're doing and you get out of their way. It's going to be about the concept of deep democracy and listening to the teams. And people will not be getting leadership roles because they have strong technical expertise but because they are purpose-led and human-focused." (Expert #11)

A central issue was the need to promote connection with emotional sensing and attuning for future leadership:

- "I don't think there will be annual reviews anymore. What we need is leaders that are extremely adaptable and have high EQ and are very good at sensing the environment." (Participant #25)
- "Some of the best leaders that I've worked with could read body language and understand how people are feeling and what impact that's having on their work and how they're doing their job. When everyone is working in a distributed manner, it will require a lot more effort from the leadership in order to plug those gaps and sense things." (Participant #21)
- "Communications skills will be more important than ever because most people will have virtual interactions before they may meet physically, so the ability to develop emotional ties over technology will be critical." (Participant #6)
- "I think with technology, which is high tech, you really need to be more high touch because it's harder to know how people are feeling and what they're thinking. So, I think the leader needs to be more grounded to figure out what people really think." (Expert #9)
- "We're going to have to be forensically attuned to the way people look and the way that they speak and the words that they choose and the presence, how they show up because the physical signals that we might see are going to be far less apparent." (Expert #6)
- "I think we'll have to play that human part a lot more in the next ten years. So, the best leader for ten years down the road is someone who can, I wouldn't say, read people's minds, but relate to people, rather than relate to decisions, spend lots of time taking care of teams' emotions." (Participant #2)

Research findings also highlighted the influence of technology in facilitating digitally enabled bonding and relationship through networking.

Participants and experts anticipated that new connected ecosystems would become more pervasive in the future:

- "The future is about being a connected ecosystem." (Participant #7)
- "It's critical that all the people in this ecosystem are sort of connected with the leader and each other." (Participant #11)
- "It's the idea that you're leading in an ecosystem that is about connection, communications networks, and pushing leadership to the edges. Leadership is no longer an activity, or a position." (Expert #13)
- "Whatever your role or your team, you will need comfort with technology because it's about the whole ecosystem that you work with. Leaders have to reshape the narrative and take ownership of the change process from where we are today to where we want to be." (Participant #27)
- "The organization can actually be a lot stronger because it's got to not just be about one or five people at the top, but it's about every single node of this very complex structure that's connected to each other like a cell structure." (Participant #10)
- "I don't think organizational leadership or global leadership will ever be the same. In fact, I think we'll see a lot more virtual connectivity in the years to come. Leadership will evolve with a lot more technology platforms, artificial intelligence, and blockchain, for example." (Expert #1)
- "For me, the progression of the idea around swarm is to think of it in terms of network and sense-making network. The traditional idea of how things are done in the organization is that the leader usually is an alpha leader with some kind of idea or point of direction. And this idea gets rolled down, and everybody is given tasks and targets around it. And that, to me is the problem because I think it starts the wrong way around. So, what I'm trying to explore is the idea of having these emerging pockets of what I'm calling 'swarm activity' where the structure of the decision-making is around the network; so, you have a business intelligence network filtered through technology. And you build that business intelligence network over time, and you have an emergent resource that anytime that you can tap into." (Expert #4)
- "It reminds me of the flocks of birds that move in these intricate patterns. It's not like geese that fly in the structured V shape. It's actually a big flock of birds with no apparent leader, but you know that there's something guiding them because they move in these very intricate patterns. And it's called a murmuration. So, I think of this image for the future of leadership. I think that as we get more and more interconnected and work with larger groups of people, this murmuration concept of purposeful, directed, but fluid collective movement will occur. It is where we're moving towards, the leadership murmuration." (Participant #25)

New End Game for Leadership

Participants and experts indicated that they were seeking a different end game from leadership. This goal was not defined according to traditional leadership models (i.e., efficiency), performance, or transformational leadership (i.e., motivation through moral uplifting). According to participants, the end game of the new leadership phenomenon was to make sense of the world collectively and derive a greater social purpose from business activity. Book titles included:

- "Leadership for good." (Participant #1)
- "Leadership for a shared purpose." (Participant #2)
- "Leadership for purpose and human bond." (Participant #13)
- "Purposeful leadership." (Participant #19)
- "Leadership for common purpose and equality." (Participant #15)
- "Purpose-led and human-focused leadership." (Participant #26)

Rather than individual competencies, participants aspired for the future of leadership to bring a new point of view on the world:

- "I think societal impact and purpose are no more 'nice to have'; they are going to be very fundamental to the future of leadership." (Participant #2)
- "Neutrality is no longer tolerated. People question, 'What do you stand for?' So, I think that leadership neutrality is no longer allowed. Consumers and people are impatient and fed up, and they want ethical leadership, and they want values-based leadership." (Participant #5)
- "The first thing a leader should look at is what is the greater good? I think you can't be a leader in the future and not be responsible for the greater good." (Participant #5)
- "In the future, the purpose and cause will matter more and be more important than the personal figure leading." (Participant #29)

Experts took the analysis a step further, characterizing the future of leadership as a means to achieve the existential purpose of connected humanity. New leadership approaches challenged the standard view of human consciousness as a first-person and singular experience and proposed that leadership become a form of extended collective consciousness and inter-brain connection:

- "Let's say we use Kegan's levels of consciousness development model. You need to be operating on a creative level rather than at a reactive level so that you are no longer self-authoring. And there's a level higher than that, of course, which is sort of an integral level which is rare, and once you're there, then you've got a fighting chance to change leadership." (Expert #6)

- "The collective brain is more efficient, more effective than the single brain. In terms of business, we're not a superorganism yet. That, to me, is the end game of connectivity and hyper connection because I'd like to see in 100 years, this idea of organizations with these interconnected networks will make up a business super organism where they truly see the value of connectivity over individual efforts and performance." (Expert #4)

A Leadership Renaissance

Thinking about the future of Asian leadership, participants and experts were bullish about Asia's role in leading a leadership renaissance:

- "The timing, I think, is right. You know, I think it's a moment of reckoning for Asia for it to be bigger in the scheme of things. Leadership does not belong to America." (Participant #14)
- "I think there is a great opportunity for leadership in Asia. In Chinese, we say 危机, which means that a crisis also brings opportunity." (Participant #26)

They believed that Asian leaders and their teams could be at the forefront of a new genre of leadership that would be more collective, digitally connected, and purposeful:

- "We're resetting the leadership mindset because Asian culture can be very collaborative, you know, friendly. So, if we set this up right, it could actually be a new model; it's the new Asian way." (Participant #2)
- "Asia has a lot of talent but not enough confidence. In contrast, America has too much confidence and not enough talent. Leadership needs more representation." (Participant #3)
- "I personally feel that a lot more could be done out of this region, especially because we know growth is out of here; we know the economic recovery is going to first come out of this region. So, leadership should not just stay in where it's traditionally headquartered but be based on where we plan to operate and where we plan to make the profit." (Participant #4)
- "In Asia, there's a lot of leading by scale. Jack Ma as a leader had a huge influence in China with the economy and e-commerce. The whole infrastructure technology has that scale to connect the dots and influence a whole new generation. I think it's quite a phenomenon." (Participant #11)

- "Asia needs to take the forefront of leadership because look at how they handled this COVID crisis. And they did a very good job with it, especially Jack Ma, this young Chinese leader who is helping countries around the world with masks and gowns. So, if there's a shift going on, then leadership could be going from the West to Asia." (Expert #5)
- "The future of leadership will be about the rise of Asia. I think for the longest period of time, we had large MNCs based in the West and Silicon Valley, pretty much leading the pack. I think that's going to change, and Asia is going to change a lot of it. A lot of these newer generation companies are going to be in Asia, like Alibaba, with different values and attention paid to how they work and lead with teams." (Participant #23)

Undeniably, Asian leaders and their teams interviewed in this study were preparing for the future. They should be considered changemakers and early adopters of a new genre of leadership, which they believe is raising the floor on our current practices and expectations of work, colleagues, and society. This networked leadership phenomenon, described by some as "Leadership on a blockchain," provides a vivid new mental picture for leadership in the next era (see Figure 8.1).

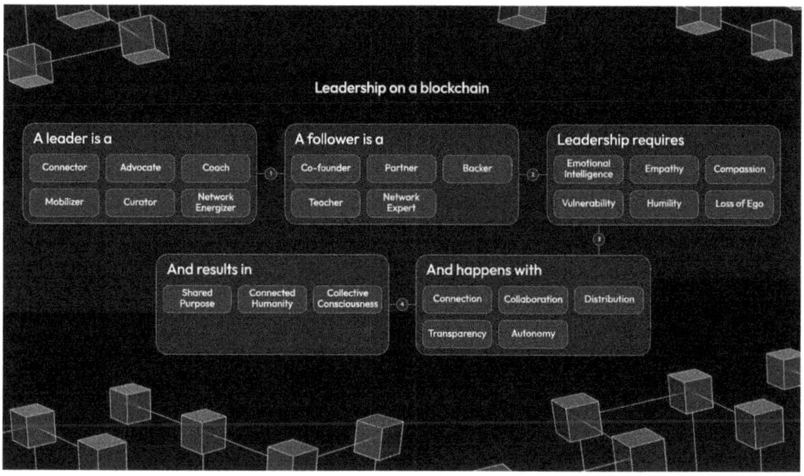

Figure 8.1 Leadership Manifesto for the Digital Age.

Source: Photo by Jeremy Bishop on Unsplash https://unsplash.com/photos/IlUq1ruyv0Q. Design by Gabriel Corbett.

9 Practitioner Starter Kit

As demonstrated in the previous chapters, leadership is rapidly transforming and offers new perspectives on the nature of work, collaboration, and our greater humanity. New language, practices, and processes challenge conventional "truths" about the protagonists of leadership – so-called "leaders and followers" – the way they interact and their motives. These ideas are exciting and promising. However, the material herein can only be helpful, scaled, and effective in providing actionable insights if organizations, leaders, and team members accept that there is a different path to leadership and want to facilitate a more significant overhaul together. The research participants in this study demonstrated an early adopter mindset that can be hard to emulate, given (1) the legacy of the hero-centric leadership literature, (2) the dominant Western-centric leadership discourse, and (3) the traditional language and imagery that have defined the field of leadership for decades. In the words of Einstein, "No problem can be solved from the same level of consciousness that created it" (Wheatley, 1999, p. 7).

It is time for a new ontological and epistemological perspective arising from leadership in Asia that challenges the Newtonian mechanistic world order in favor of a community-oriented understanding. We must also transcend the Cartesian division of parts thinking and embrace the interconnectedness of life to envision leadership as a connected human process of flow and connection. While the emerging literature on learning has integrated the advances of the digital age in knowledge creation and organizational design with networked approaches, the field of leadership is still far behind. Fundamentally, the hope is that this material can help raise new questions on the "what, how, and why" of leadership to help business practitioners and those they work with (regardless of where they come from and practice) foster new leadership capacity and inspire change.

DOI: 10.4324/9781003399377-18

Developing a Team-Based Mental Model of Leadership

According to Forbes (Westfall, 2019), the leadership development industry is worth $366 billion globally, with an estimated $166 billion spent annually on leadership development in the United States alone. The field is hugely prolific, with nearly 95% of learning organizations planning to increase or maintain their current investment in leadership development (Prokopeak, 2018). Yet, Conger (2014) has documented that leadership development has been hit or miss in most organizations that lack dedicated and consistent training with rigorous evaluation assessments. Over a decade ago, Hollenbeck and McCall (2003) asserted that global executive development had not worked due to outdated approaches focused on the heroic leader rather than relational competencies across teams. A more recent study from McKinsey (Gurdjian et al., 2014) offers startling insights into why most leadership programs fail: established leadership viewpoints that do not adapt to the context and company at hand, training that is inundated with too many concepts and scarce hands-on practice, little consideration given to the preexisting beliefs of the C-suite that become obstacles to change, and an overall lack of leadership measurement.

To identify the "adjacent possible" (Kauffmann, 1996) of leadership – or in other words, the most realistic set of possibilities available to practitioners for driving change and evolving leadership practices – it is essential to embrace a team-based mental model for leadership. The proposed framework is a deliberate attempt to align leadership development to team-based learning instead of individual skills that only further reinforce the heroic view of leadership. Training and methods that focus on leader competencies are bound to fail as they fundamentally ignore the entire leadership journey and the interactions at the core of the leadership dynamic (organizational structures, teams, values, behaviors, relationship development, etc.). According to Klimoski and Mohammed (1994), "team mental models are team members' shared, organized understanding and mental representation of knowledge about key elements of the team's relevant environment" (Mohammed & Dumville, 2001, p. 90).

A shared "team-based mental model" needs to be developed for leadership based on the three types of knowledge to be recast (Converse & Kahler, 1992):

1 Declarative knowledge – implications on changing *what* leadership is
2 Procedural knowledge – implications on *how* leadership is enacted
3 Strategic knowledge – implications on *why* leadership matters.

First, it is critical to foster a new shared team mental model of what leadership is so the leadership iconography can evolve. Practitioners are encouraged to use a Socratic method to facilitate cooperative dialogue on what leadership is today and what it can become in the future in their work context. Asking and answering questions to stimulate critical thinking on the nature of leadership and whom it will involve can help draw out new ideas and possibilities while addressing underlying presuppositions. Using new leadership language discovered in this study to displace the legacy of "leaders" and "followers" can be helpful to present leadership in a novel way and institute new declarative knowledge. Focusing on the new actors involved in the leadership dynamic, the relationships between them, and the networks to be built can bring a more holistic perspective to the conversation on leadership (see Figure 9.1, top section).

Second, a shared team mental model of how leadership is enacted must be discussed and developed. New leadership behaviors should be examined beyond the typical expectations of control, power, and influence by those who are in the working group. Teams must establish the landscape of the connections and contributions they aim to gain from leadership, exploring new areas such as learning and emotional connections (see Figure 9.1, middle section).

Finally, a shared team mental model of why leadership is being developed is paramount, as questioning leadership outcomes is critical. Discussing and co-creating the unseen connections formed by the leadership process and exploring the greater meaning of leadership, its purpose, and contributions to the organization, employees, community, and greater society will allow a richer reflection on the goals and possible networked effect of the leadership enacted. It will help all those involved discuss why leadership matters and is a far more meaningful endeavor than a singular first-person business management exercise (see Figure 9.1, bottom section).

Challenging what leadership looks like, sounds like, feels like, and why it matters is everyone's responsibility. We all play an essential role in setting the direction for leadership and establishing the standards for practice, training, and development. Practitioners constitute both the demand and supplier sides of the equation; therefore, they must challenge established norms and provide new case studies for academic literature. Drawing from 14 years of published research from 2000 to 2013, Meuser et al. (2016) discovered that only six leadership approaches appeared as the focal point of leadership theory and learning: transformational leadership, charismatic leadership, strategic leadership, leadership and diversity, participative/shared leadership, and the trait approach to leadership. Practitioners should encourage greater diversity in the study and practice of leadership to end its reductionist approach. The language of leadership weighs heavily on the expressed concepts, images, and emotions they carry. Practitioners

Study Implications For Practitioners

	Current Questions	→ New Questions	
	Leadership Iconography		
Declarative Knowledge *What is leadership*	• Who is the leader/person/individual/ in charge of this team? • How senior is the leader? • What are his/her credentials? • Who will the leader report to? • Who are the subordinates? • Who are the direct reports? • Who are the followers? • Who sits at the top of the org chart?	• Who are the people needed to connect on this team/project? • How strong are their bonds? • What domain experts are needed? • Who are the mobilizers? • Who are the cofounders? • Who are the teachers? • Who are the extended members? • What networks do we need to build and connect for success?	New Understanding of Leadership
	Leadership Behaviors		
Procedural Knowledge *How is Leadership Enacted*	• Who is leading? • Who is directing? • Who is deciding? • Who is influencing? • Who is persuading? • Who has the power over others? • Who is communicating?	• With whom and how will we learn? • With whom and how will we connect? • With whom and how will we energize? • With whom and how will we sense the environment? • With whom and how will we share power? • With whom and how will we attune to each other?	New Practices and Leadership Process
	Leadership Outcomes		
Strategic Knowledge *Why Leadership matters*	• What do we want to control? • What are we conditioning for? • What goals do we need to align everyone to? • How do we end up on top?	• What connected experience do we want to achieve? • What purpose are we striving for? • What is the force for good we aim to create with our work and leadership?	New End Game of Leadership

Figure 9.1 Study Implications for Practitioners.

must help reframe leadership through new semantic and syntactic representations reflecting their actual work product and new possibilities.

Encouraging Decentralized Organizational Governance

Aside from those involved in the leadership dynamic, what can be done to re-architect companies for better leadership? According to Steward (2022), it is time to stop developing leaders and start developing leadership at the company level instead. He argues for the importance of making leadership an organizational competency and an equal opportunity right for all workers regardless of their level, title, and their number of reports. At its basic level, "leadership is creating the conditions for an organization (and the people within it) to fulfill its potential" (Steward, 2022, "What's Leadership, Anyway?" section). Leadership on a blockchain requires more than a philosophy and practice; it also needs an effective governance ecosystem and a departure from the traditional structure of the firm as we have known it for the last century. Blockchain experts Don and Alex Tapscott (2018) contend that a blockchain revolution is happening and that, eventually, the world will shift toward a blockchain economy reinventing financial services, rebuilding government and democracy, freeing culture, and re-architecting the firm itself. Tapscott and Tapscott argue that we need to change the boundaries of the firm and "leverage blockchain technologies to distribute power, increase transparency, respect user privacy and anonymity" (2018, p. 92).

While the seventeenth century gave rise to the joint-stock company, and the nineteenth century helped the development of limited liability, the proliferation of the internet has not yet been fully leveraged to drive organizational and leadership innovation. Although today's internet and expanding Web3 technologies based on decentralization, blockchain technologies, and token-based economics can enable radical openness and new opportunities for partnerships and connectivity, the control of companies remains highly concentrated. Corporate boards, proprietary intellectual property, talent management, hierarchy, and salary grids are all evidence of the corporate concentration of power. Centralized governance has made possible the creation of some of the most powerful enterprises in history but also put a small minority in charge and created an elite class of workers, who are most often referred to as the "leaders." A new form of corporate governance, which does not rely on management, centralized leadership, or formal legal structures, can change this; it is called the "decentralized autonomous organization" (DAO).

According to the World Economic Forum (2022, p. 6), a "Decentralized Autonomous Organization (DAO) is a general term for a group that uses blockchains and related technologies to coordinate its activities." Popular DAO platforms, such as DAOstack and Aragon, define a DAO as "a network of stakeholders with no central governing body (https://daostack.io), which is regulated by a set of automatically enforceable rules on a public blockchain" (Hassan & De Filippi, 2021, p. 4). DAOs are a new organizational form that offers the promise of decentralizing governance by empowering all members to propose, vote on, and effect changes to an entity and make decisions communally. DAOs have the following distinctive characteristics:

- Enable people to coordinate and self-govern themselves online
- Use source code deployed in a blockchain with smart contract capabilities, which specifies the rules for interaction among people
- Have a governance mechanism based on code rather than people and remain independent from central control.

Since 2016, the first DAOs have experienced explosive growth and have been deployed to support various business ideas and applications (e.g., collective investment in cryptocurrencies, community networking, crowdfunding, and ridesharing). At the core, they are less about a specific business model than supporting a fully automated decision-making process and enabling communities to work collectively toward achieving shared goals, often without top-down, hierarchal management. While still experimenting with different decision-making methods, DAOs allow more comprehensive representation by awarding all their participants – not just a few select executives – governance rights through voting tokens.

In addition, in real time, financial and operational information is accessible through public permissionless blockchains with smart contracts that can automatically execute, control, or document legally relevant events and actions. Therefore, DAOs are part of a changing logic of leadership and organizations (see Table 9.1). In the past, hierarchical management used centralization as a means of control to direct human activity. Today, corporations understand the importance of employee engagement and collaboration to scale their business but still retain tight control through legal structures such as joint-stock companies. In the future, companies will be

Table 9.1 The Changing Logic of Leadership and Organizations

Past	*Present*	*Future*
Control	Engagement	Networking
Centralization	Collaboration	Decentralization
Family and government structures	Legally registered private and public organizations	Autonomous organizations
Internal orientation	External positioning	External adaptation
Closed hierarchy	Shareholders	Network of stakeholders
Defined set of closed processes	Processes based on human relationships	Processes based on networks of partnerships and alliances
Elite governing body enforcing the rules	Distributed governing body voting on rules	No central governing body, automatically enforceable rules based on code
Generic organizational design	Contingent organizational design	Flexible and fluid network design
Organization designed around internal functions	Organization designed around externally oriented products and customers	Organization designed for external environment and rapid evolution
Value-add from management	Value-add from employees	Value-add from people who self-govern, partnerships, and alliances in the network
Management focus	Leader focus	Network focus

able to operate in a fully decentralized manner with no central governing body, using automatically enforceable rules based on code.

Although still in the early phases of development, DAOs offer the promise of prosocial goals with the desire to empower a significant number of actors in the leadership dynamic. They aim to address key governance issues such as information asymmetry, power concentration, and opaque and exclusive decision-making. DAOs are also well aligned with the transformation of leadership documented in this study, particularly the search for greater connectivity and purpose. DAOs galvanize their participants through a common purpose and leverage peer-to-peer collaboration to agree on the critical parameters of governance automated by computer code. They promote transparency and trust through technology integrity and are fundamentally at the service of a community with a leaderless approach, as everyone is accountable for their actions.

Pressure is mounting to replace closed business architectures that reinforce hierarchical models of power and wealth with new ways to govern resources and human capital. Henceforth, substantial research is underway to discover new approaches to decentralized governance leveraging blockchain ecosystems. The Blockchain Research Institute (2022) has been a leading voice on the topic, exploring new models of engagement, execution, and trust. Their research team has proposed a new stewardship model called *decentralized resource governance* (DRG). A project can be run end to end using a DRG to guide resource allocation, funding, communication, decision-making, and dispute resolution, proving that decentralization does not inevitably lead to total disorganization and chaos. The DRG model is guided by four principles, including (1) having a strong community vision guiding the enterprise and its stakeholders, (2) ensuring a balanced distribution of power, (3) guaranteeing the transparency of decision-making mechanisms, and (4) maintaining operational stability (Blockchain Research Institute, 2022).

Understanding the Repercussions of Blockchain on Organizations

Theodore C. Chartier-Rueg and Thomas David Zweifel (2017) propose that the repercussions of the adoption of blockchain technology on organizations will be extremely significant, enabling the distribution of power and authority, peer-to-peer collaboration, performance-based remuneration, task decentralization, agility, and automation. His conclusive evaluation of the leadership implications is that every member of the organization will have more authority and decision power than ever before, along with greater access to information. This will drastically affect the role of leaders as "the shift towards a blockchain infrastructure will force managers to acknowledge they are intermediaries instead of agents" (Chartier-Rueg & Zweifel, 2017, p. 18).

Groysberg and Slind (2012) describe five long-term business trends that require a reappraisal of leadership conversations in organizations: (1) economic change (shift toward service industries), (2) organizational change (flatter and less hierarchical structure), (3) global change (higher diversity making communication harder within the organization), (4) generational change (new generations expecting more dynamic and peer-to-peer interactions), and (5) technological change (instant connectivity as the norm). Progressive Asian leaders and their teams are already making the shift toward networked leadership, answering these changes in their everyday practices. The move toward a blockchain future is in line with these new conditions accelerating the human transformation toward leadership on a blockchain.

In conclusion, this practitioners' starter kit encourages leaders and team members to arm themselves with the knowledge of this research and to be actors of change. As leaders come to terms with the need for greater transparency, trust, adaptability, and speed, they need to look at the entire apparatus of leadership:

- Themselves – accept the loss of the heroic leader figure and the ego of leadership
- Their teams – recognize their teammates as domain experts, teachers, and equal partners in the leadership dynamic and journey
- The governance structure that holds the business activity – experiment with more open and distributed corporate governance systems
- The collective ambition for leadership – articulate the impact of the business activity on people, communities, and society in human terms, not just economic.

References

Blockchain Research Institute. (2022). *Decentralized resource governance a new model of engagement, execution, and trust.* https://www.blockchainresearchinstitute.org/project/decentralized-resource-governance/

Chartier-Rueg, T. C. & Zweifel, T. D. (2017) Leadership and management: Business as usual or radical disruption? *Eureka: Social and Humanities*, *4*, 76–110. https://doi.org/10.21303/2504–5571.2017.00370

Conger, J. A. (July 01, 2014). Addressing the organizational barriers to developing global leadership talent. *Organizational Dynamics, 43*(3), 198–204.

Converse, S. A., & Kahler, S. E. (1992). *Knowledge acquisition and the measurement of shared mental models.* Naval Training Systems Center.

Groysberg, B., & Slind, M. (2012). Leadership is a conversation. *Harvard Business Review*, *90*(6), 76–84.

Gurdjian, P., Halbeisen, T., & Lane, K. (2014, January 1). *Why leadership-development programs fail*. McKinsey & Company. https://www.mckinsey.com/featured-insights/leadership/why-leadership-development-programs-fail

Hassan, S., & De Filippi, P. (2021). Decentralized autonomous organization. *Internet Policy Review*, *10*(2), 2–10.

Hollenbeck, G. P., & McCall, M. W. (2003). Competence, not competencies: Making global executive development work. *Advances in Global Leadership*, *3*(101), 101–119. https://doi.org/10.1016/S1535-1203(02)03005-8.

Kauffmann, S. (1996). *At home in the universe: The search for the laws of self-organization and complexity*. Oxford University Press.

Klimoski, R., & Mohammed, S. (1994). Team mental model: Construct or metaphor? *Journal of Management*, *20*, 403–437. https://doi.org/10.1016/0149-2063(94)90021-3

Meuser, J. D., Gardner, W. L., Dinh, J. E., Hu, J., Liden, R. C., & Lord, R. G. (2016). A network analysis of leadership theory: The infancy of integration. *Journal of Management*. https://doi.org/10.1177/0149206316647099

Mohammed, S., & Dumville, B. C. (2001). Team mental models in a team knowledge framework: Expanding theory and measurement across disciplinary boundaries. *Journal of Organizational Behavior*, *22*, 89–106. https://onlinelibrary.wiley.com/doi/epdf /10.1002/job.86

Prokopeak, M. (2018, March 21). *Follow the leader(ship) spending*. Chief Learning Officer Business Intelligence Board. https://www.chieflearningofficer.com/2018/03/21/follow-the-leadership-spending/

Steward, A. (2022, January 21). *Why it's time to stop developing leaders: We need to start developing leadership instead*. Medium. https://medium.com/the-ready/why-its-time-to-stop-developing-leaders-dae0edb80bff

Tapscott, D., & Tapscott, A. (2018). *Blockchain revolution: How the technology behind bitcoin and other cryptocurrencies is changing the world*. Portfolio.

Westfall, C. (2019, June 20). *Leadership development is a $366 billion industry: Here's why most programs don't work*. Forbes. https://www.forbes.com/sites/chriswestfall/2019/06/20/leadership-development-why-most-programs-dont-work/?sh=4801121361de

Wheatley, M. J. (1999). *Leadership and the new science: Discovering order in a chaotic world* (2nd ed.). Berrett-Koehler Publishers.

World Economic Forum. (2022, June 23). *Decentralized autonomous organizations: Beyond the hype*. https://www.weforum.org/whitepapers/decentralized-autonomous-organizations-beyond-the-hype/

Part III
Conclusion

Conclusion

This part distilled the critical lessons that global leaders can take from the research learnings.

A summary of leadership's inflection points in the last decade was proposed along with two meta-themes – connectivity and purpose – to ground the evolving leadership construct.

A description of the changing roles of leaders (as relationship brokers, advocates, coaches, and mobilizers) and of followers (as cofounders, domain experts, and teachers) was provided along with new language to recognize the importance of partnerships, empowerment, teams, and networks in the new relational dynamic at play.

A leadership manifesto for the digital age detailed how leadership on a blockchain embodies a new philosophy and reinvents leadership understanding, practices, processes, goals, and norms. Finally, practitioners were provided with a starter kit on how to lead a revolution in leadership in their own organizations.

DOI: 10.4324/9781003399377-19

Conclusion

The fundamental failing of leadership is inherent in its etymology – "leader-ship" – which narrowly defines and constructs the concept from a singular person's perspective. From the outset, the term presents an asymmetric relationship between the participants involved in the leadership dynamic, suggesting that an individual leader is solely responsible for the fullness of a collective process by adding a noun suffix. This misleading idea has been perpetuated for centuries, galvanized by heroic leadership literature, debunked research theories on "great men," ideals of Western-centric philosophy promoting individualism, and the mythological symbolism of the heroic pioneer in America. This book demonstrates that most of these ideas can be challenged – if not retired – due to a radical transformation of leadership in the last decade and the accelerated pace of change since the global pandemic. According to *Harvard Business Review*,

> the traditional model of the leader-hero who saves the day, knows it all, is the smartest person in the room, and is too often driven by power, fame, glory, or money is not appropriate in today's environment. People today expect a different kind of leader.
>
> (Joly, 2022)

It is time to change what leadership looks, sounds, and feels like and make it matter to *everyone*. I beg my peers to stop publishing more leadership books and frameworks such as "the 4 C's" or "the 5 Ps" on first-person skills and competencies. As Richard Kelly (2019, p. 69) aptly put it, we need to urgently transition our thinking "from Egosystems to Ecosystems." This research has offered a compelling perspective on new practices arising from Asia and ideas we can take forward for the future. By proposing to view leadership on a blockchain, some new business fundamentals emerge:

DOI: 10.4324/9781003399377-20

- Distributed power, decentralized governance, transparency, adaptability, and speed are the new parameters for business success.

  The global pandemic has accelerated the increasingly complex, challenging, and uncertain business environment; there is now an urgency for agility, adaptability, and transformation. As a result, work practices must adjust to deal with faster economic cycles, a shortage of capital investment, contracting Gross Domestic Product (GDP) growth, and fluctuating consumer confidence. Gone are the days of long-term planning and work assigned by titles and delineated roles. Businesses need to operate in a hyper volatility, uncertainty, complexity and ambiguity (VUCA) world (Bennis & Nanus, 1985) and embrace "Super-Flexibility for Real-Time Adaptation" (Bahrami & Evans, 2011). Everyone on a team must be hands-on, frequently monitoring and shifting competitive strategies, constantly connected to colleagues and customers, promoting open information flows, and operating from a peer-to-peer and co-founder mindset.

- It is time to give power to others.

  As younger workers enter the workforce, they have radically different expectations of their relationships with managers and co-workers. They expect to have a voice and the ability to influence decisions equally. Power is no longer seen as a privilege based on seniority, title, or salary. It is not only the younger generation; the global pandemic has changed workers of all ages. More people are hedging on returning to the office full-time as they re-evaluate what "work" means to them. This is not just a preference for "where" the business activity occurs but "how" and the advent of new power dynamics. Many workers have developed a form of "leadership immunity" – a resistance to being subjected to the power of their manager and an aversion to being treated as "followers." New levels of autonomy and personal agency have become net new gains from the remote economy, and they are here to stay.

- Trust is the new business protocol.

  In a world of declining trust in institutions, government, business, media, and technology, trust has become one of the most precious and rare values of human exchange. Organizations need to think of trust as the *sine qua non* of all their activities – how they hire, train, and manage teams; how they enable peers to network and collaborate; and how they create secure and open access to information, capital, and voting rights. The business world is reckoning with a new social contract that runs on a trust protocol and begets new values such as authenticity, honesty, and integrity. Emotion, noticeably absent from the business environment until now, is finally being recognized as a core imperative for talent management as employees seek greater engagement through a display of humility, vulnerability, compassion, and support. BBMG (2022, p.31) affirms that leadership now requires "welcoming vulnerability, embracing 'not knowing' and turning challenges into quests."

- Purpose matters.

Expectations of organizations have changed, as well as people's roles within them. The hard-charging, profit-optimizing hero-leader model has lost much of its appeal. Furthermore, making a living and having a long career have fallen to the bottom of the worker's Maslow pyramid. The unprecedented shock of the global pandemic has accelerated the search for purpose and placed it at the very top of the hierarchy of needs for human self-actualization. Faced with harsher realities of social injustice, discrimination, gender tensions, economic crisis, and environmental change, there is a broader reappraisal of the meaning of life and the contribution of organizations. Companies are increasingly challenged by their roles in society. According to Derek O'Halloran from the World Economic Forum, 64% of employees expect their Chief Executive Officer (CEO) to take a leading role in tackling a societal challenge, and 74% expect their CEO to explain and demonstrate what they have done to help make the world become a better place (World Economic Forum, 2022). Companies and teams need to state and abide by a purpose that is materially greater than merely making money.

These are exciting times to reclaim what humans do best – meaning-making from their social and business activities. I propose we retire the word "leader-ship" and introduce the concept of "network-ship" to usher in a new worldview of leadership based on connectivity, fairness, and justice. Changing thinking on a broad cultural level for leadership is necessary, and we must radically rewrite the rules of how we can collaborate and create societal responsibility. Networkship is not just the recognition that 70% of the new values created in the economy over the next decade will be based on digitally networked business models (World Economic Forum, 2022). It is also the belief that we can create a human-centered ethos – of building connections, learning together, and co-creating change – to produce results that far exceed any individual's contribution. We must recognize, accept, and celebrate that we are profoundly interconnected and that our potential can only be realized if it is truly integrated. Every person thrives in taking part in a larger whole. We need to focus the next stage of our civilization on distributed cognition, which unleashes the effects of thinking *with* and *through* others so we can coordinate multiple areas of knowledge and expertise, harness collective intelligence, and connect our mental states into a sum total to feel our way to the richness, meaning, and evolution. Leadership on a blockchain communicates a new visual possibility for people to shift from a system based on domination to one of trust, partnership, and connectedness, where each of us comprises the human blocks of the chain that will change the future.

References

Bahrami, H., & Evans, S. (2011). Super-flexibility for real-time adaptation: Perspectives from Silicon Valley. *California Management Review*, *53*(3), 21–39. https://cmr.berkeley.edu/search/articleDetail.aspx?article=5633

BBMG. (2022, June 7). *Leading regenerative brands*. https://bbmg.com/leading-regenerative-brands/

Bennis, W., & Nanus, B. (1985). *Leaders: Strategies for taking charge*. Harper & Row.

Joly, H. (2022). *5 principles of purposeful leadership*. Harvard Business Review. https://hbr.org/2022/04/5-principles-of-purposeful-leadership

Kelly, R. (2019). *Constructing leadership 4.0: Swarm leadership and the fourth industrial revolution*. Palgrave Macmillan.

World Economic Forum. (2022). *Platforms: Shaping the future of digital economy and new value creation*. https://www.weforum.org/platforms/shaping-the-future-of-digital-economy-and-new-value-creation

Index

Note: **Bold** page numbers refer to tables and *italic* page numbers refer to figures.

For Product Safety Concerns and Information please contact our EU representative GPSR@taylorandfrancis.com
Taylor & Francis Verlag GmbH, Kaufingerstraße 24, 80331 München, Germany

www.ingramcontent.com/pod-product-compliance
Ingram Content Group UK Ltd.
Pitfield, Milton Keynes, MK11 3LW, UK
UKHW022354190926
475702UK00015B/2286
* 9 7 8 1 0 3 2 5 0 6 3 1 9 *